AF361573

UNDERSTANDING
BARBARA KINGSOLVER

UNDERSTANDING CONTEMPORARY AMERICAN LITERATURE
Matthew J. Bruccoli, Founding Editor
Linda Wagner-Martin, Series Editor

Also of Interest

UNDERSTANDING

BARBARA KINGSOLVER

Ian Tan

THE UNIVERSITY OF
SOUTH CAROLINA PRESS

© 2024 University of South Carolina

Published by the University of South Carolina Press
Columbia, South Carolina 29208

uscpress.com

Printed in the United States of America

Library of Congress Cataloging-in-Publication Data
can be found at https://lccn.loc.gov/2023054093

ISBN: 978-1-64336-476-6 (hardcover)
ISBN: 978-1-64336-477-3 (paperback)
ISBN: 978-1-64336-478-0 (ebook)

CONTENTS

SERIES EDITOR'S PREFACE

The Understanding Contemporary American Literature series was founded by the estimable Matthew J. Bruccoli (1931–2008), who envisioned these volumes as guides or companions for students as well as good nonacademic readers, a legacy that will continue as new volumes are developed to fill in gaps among the nearly one hundred series volumes published to date and to embrace a host of new writers only now making their marks on our literature.

As Professor Bruccoli explained in his preface to the volumes he edited, because much influential contemporary literature makes special demands, "the word *understanding* in the titles was chosen deliberately. Many willing readers lack an adequate understanding of how contemporary literature works; that is, of what the author is attempting to express and the means by which it is conveyed." Aimed at fostering this understanding of good literature and good writers, the criticism and analysis in the series provide instruction in how to read certain contemporary writers—explicating their material, language, structures, themes, and perspectives—and facilitate a more profitable experience of the works under discussion.

In the twenty-first century, Professor Bruccoli's prescience gives us an avenue to publish expert critiques of significant contemporary American writing. The series continues to map the literary landscape and to provide both instruction and enjoyment. Future volumes will seek to introduce new voices alongside canonized favorites, to chronicle the changing literature of our times, and to remain, as Professor Bruccoli conceived, contemporary in the best sense of the word.

Linda Wagner-Martin, Series Editor

ACKNOWLEDGMENTS

Research for this book has been made possible by a research grant given by the National Institute of Education, Nanyang Technological University. My special thanks to the English Language and Literature Academic Group for supporting me in the writing of this book, and to Ms. Megan Sin for her assistance.

ABBREVIATIONS

AD	*Animal Dreams*
AVM	*Animal, Vegetable, Miracle: A Year of Food Life*
BT	*The Bean Trees*
DC	*Demon Copperhead*
FB	*Flight Behavior*
HT	*High Tide in Tucson*
L	*The Lacuna*
PB	*The Poisonwood Bible*
PH	*Pigs in Heaven*
PS	*Prodigal Summer*
SW	*Small Wonder: Essays*
U	*Unsheltered*

CHAPTER 1

Understanding Barbara Kingsolver

Barbara Kingsolver's fictional output has consolidated her reputation as one of the most compelling and relevant artistic voices working in the English language, with the most recent distinction coming as the Pulitzer Prize for Fiction for *Demon Copperhead* in 2023. The critical aims of this study will be to delineate the major thematic concerns underpinning the range of Kingsolver's novelistic work, from this latest prize-winning novel to *The Bean Trees*. I will focus on her abiding interests in using the fictional perspective as a much-needed corrective against the domination of heteronormative ways of viewing societies, bodies, and the environment. So deeply is her investment in reclaiming alternative modes of coexistence embedded throughout her novels that her fiction becomes a vehicle for raising awareness against the literal and symbolic violence that capitalistic economy and patriarchy have unfortunately inscribed on our collective psyches as the price for the developments associated with modernity. To understand Kingsolver's ethical employment of her characters and concerns is to understand the ways through which *difference* allows ossified distinctions between the human and nonhuman, cultural construction and natural immanence to break down. The familiar once again becomes unfamiliar and worthy of consideration.

In Kingsolver's hands narrative does not serve to erect a linguistic barrier between the human being, whose access to language confirms his or her anthropocentric mastery, and the muteness of nature that renders it vulnerable to domination and exploitation. Instead, the literary text bears witness to an "ever-unfolding story" wherein "we—along with the other animals, plants and landforms—are all characters" (Abram 270). As we see it worked out in her fiction, the dynamism of this biological embeddedness does not imply that tensions between the human and the animal, language and reality can be smoothed out into an artificial vision of unity that neglects to consider the historical consequences and legacies of violence. Kingsolver's ethical orientation harnesses difference as a creative tensional *becoming* that allows renewal from within—the solicitation to her reader is always to understand the same as different. As Bonnie Costello argues, "criticism can involve real-world concerns in that it reveals the entanglement of nature and culture, the interplay between our desires, our concepts, and our perceptions, and possibilities for renewal and vitality within that entanglement" (14). To develop Costello's observation, I will argue that it is in the juxtaposition between perception—what life under the conditions of advanced capitalism presents to consciousness—and concepts—what life could be like as dignified ethical and political practice— that Kingsolver's utopian writerly practice resides.

Kingsolver's biography helps place the significance that cultural difference played in her formative years as a writer. Born in 1955 to Wendell Kingsolver and Virginia Lee Henry, Barbara's father combined his professional knowledge as a medical doctor and idealism in choosing to serve the under-resourced people of Nicholas County, Kentucky. This personal mission to provide modern medical assistance to the poor led the family to live in the Congo for several years while Dr. Kingsolver worked in the area as part of a medical mission. Barbara's respect for her father is clearly enunciated in a 2003 interview with Linda Wagner-Martin; as Wagner-Martin observes, she learns from her father a form of practical idealism, using his craft and knowledge "to matter in the world" (*Barbara Kingsolver* 6). We may likewise suitably characterize Barbara Kingsolver's fiction as being driven by an impetus to make literature matter, in that it employs the linguistic medium in order to enact a paradigmatic shift in our understanding of place and identity. Kingsolver's own time in Africa also primed her to appreciate the conceptual shifts necessary for understanding diversity and difference as modes of readjusting American exceptionalism and privilege. As Wagner-Martin writes, "one of the wisest observations King-solver makes in the process of her emphasizing the benevolence of the African children—accepting as they were of the strange-looking Americans—was that the idea of normality itself was a cultural construct" (*Barbara Kingsolver* 18). What precipitates for her is an uncanny moment of defamiliarization, where the self becomes "othered" and "decentered" through the gaze of the person who is different from the subject. We can note here that Kingsolver's fiction enacts this same dynamism of "othering," wherein literary language translates the experiences of the reader by placing him or her in immediate contact with perspectives that are not their own.

Indeed, Kingsolver's ironic transcription of her family's experiences in the Congo in *The Poisonwood Bible* pits intolerance against accommodation, arguing for a subject position not only vulnerable enough to acknowledge the dominant culture's culpability in exploiting the resources of the voiceless, but also resilient enough to transform various traumatic encounters with otherness into more fluid, nonhierarchical definitions of selfhood. As Hubert Zapf writes, Kingsolver's work is framed by a textual ecology of interchangeable subject positions, one "which constantly transgresses and shifts the boundaries of what can be known, said, and thought within a culture by opening them towards their excluded other, which remains unknowable, unsayable, and unthinkable within its rules of discourse" (61): the egotism of the self is constantly undercut by literary language's ability to inhabit and validate different centers of value, thereby undermining cultural normativity.

Kingsolver's itinerant inclination sets up a paradoxical understanding of selfhood being necessarily different from itself within an untotalizable woof or nexus of relationships. Wagner-Martin details how traveling became important for the writer during her university days: "the simple act of moving to new terrain, surrounding herself with unknown people and then making a place for herself, became a definition of the power of the self" (*Barbara Kingsolver* 38). Relocating from Kentucky to Tucson, Arizona, switching her course of study from music to biology, the changes in Kingsolver's life provided her with ways to encounter difference as rescuing a precious particularity of place. Her novelistic vision is suitably informed by an ecocritical stance that presses "against modernist abstract universalism [in order to bring attention to] the value of life as embodied and embedded, situated and engaged, local and particular" (Curry 98). Living and consuming sustainably, as she details in *Animal, Vegetable, Miracle*, is not only about an ethical response to the excesses of consumerism, but also putting an ecocritical understanding of place *into practice*. The next part of this introductory chapter explores the significance of ecocriticism to Kingsolver, placing theoretical arguments in the ecocritical literature together with some of Kingsolver's major themes. This will set the stage for the detailed literary analyses the rest of the book will outline.

Ecocriticism, Literary Strategy, and the Ethics of Kingsolver's Fiction

Ecocritical theory combines nonhierarchical patterns of understanding relationships within the ecosphere with a concern for the ways in which literature engages with "external reality." Ecocriticism attempts to respond to the reality of the Anthropocene, characterized by Timothy Clark as naming "a kind of threshold at which modes of thinking and practices that were once self-evidently adequate, progressive or merely innocuous become . . . latently destructive" (*Ecocriticism* 21). It urges a rethinking of all aspects of our political, economic, and cultural transactions with the biosphere. The effect of anthropogenetic pressures of the environment precipitates a crisis-situation wherein old modes of literary representation need to be reevaluated. This tipping point, wherein humanity is faced with choices and decisions that could bring about unmitigated catastrophe, enjoins us to inhabit new representational frameworks that are sensitive to the ways in which environmental degradation has impacted biological life on multiple levels. As Greg Garrard writes, "none of the traditional forms in literature, film, or television documentary is unproblematically suited to capturing the geographical and temporal scale, complexity, and uncertainty of climate change" (709). New modes of literary criticism that interrogate the limits and boundaries of representing the "environment" thereby puts traditional conceptual hierarchies in question, with the divide between the human and the nonhuman being subject to the most scrutiny.

Indeed, ecocriticism takes as its ethical focus the fact that "the current environmental crisis is the troubling material expression of modern culture's philosophical assumptions, epistemological convictions, aesthetic principles, and ethical imperatives" (Gersdorf and Mayer 9): ecocritical theory offers a reassessment of the role and place of reason, human intelligence, and language, all these being modernist hallmarks of the centrality of the human animal within the ecosystem. At its very basis, ecocritical literary analysis marks the limits of anthropocentric language in texts and remodels our very relationship to nature as "the site of a constant, *creative renewal* of language, perception, communication, and imagination" (Zapf 56).

Ecocritical literary analysis then, "seeks to evaluate texts and ideas in terms of their coherence and usefulness as responses to environmental crisis" (Kerridge and Sammells 5), not in order to return literary consciousness to an uncritical "appreciation" of a uncorrupted natural realm, but to investigate the ways in which an ecological consciousness registers embeddedness and enmeshment within nature as "a kind of relationship, an achievement among many actors, not all of them human, not all of them organic" (Haraway 297). We may read Kingsolver's fiction as being heavily invested in similar ideas of contact and entanglement between the familiar and the strange: meeting-points between human and nonhuman agents across cultures and species continually offer her characters opportunities to reassess their convictions and assumptions about the ways the world works. Just as *The Poisonwood Bible* demonstrates the negative effects of imperiously imposing a set of beliefs and assumptions upon the cultural and geographical landscape, *Prodigal Summer* gently invites a redefinition of place, one that stresses how the nonhuman both functions "as a distinctive mode of being and relation" and "a powerful figure for conceiving social and political community" (Keenleyside 16–17).

For Kingsolver ecocritical consciousness defines an ethics and politics of existence. Redefining the very limits of family and community become crucial preludes to her utopian notion of coexistence, for we become stewards of the environment when we recognize how our collective histories are formed in ways that imbricate the human with the more-than-human. As Leonard Scigaj writes, ecocritical "language is often foregrounded only to reveal its limitations, and this is accomplished in such a way that the reader's gaze is thrust beyond language back into the less limited natural world that language refers to, the inhabited place where humans must live in harmony with ecological cycles" (37–38)—literature must speak of an unfolding drama of belonging wherein we all become responsible decision makers in developing and sustaining ameliorative ecological practices and politics.

The relevance of an ecocritical literary practice for Kingsolver therefore resides not so much in prescriptions about how to conserve the environment, but rather "as a way of reflecting upon what it might mean to dwell with the earth" (Bate 266). Insofar as the literary text presents this hermeneutical reading of the lived environment, it also casts self-conscious light on its status as linguistic speech act. As we read Kingsolver's novels, we are also paying attention to how she constantly explores the ways in which narrative understanding molds a different attunement toward place as existential locus—we read her with an ecocritical focus as to how "narratives shape our views of nature, and in turn, what this implies about our ways of thinking about the environment and our role in it" (Bracke 226). As Andrew McMurry succinctly notes, Kingsolver's "ecoliterate text . . . tries to describe—or inscribe—new grooves for thinking and being" (19). Just as Kingsolver's characters find themselves continually being led out of their isolation back into human sociality and a redemptive notion of community, the literary text leads toward the world it has a stake in changing. If ecocriticism "seizes opportunities offered by recent biological research to make humanistic studies more socially responsible," then Kingsolver's marrying of her training as a biologist with her novelistic craft signals a happy meeting-point between the language of the literary text and the language of reality, a rapprochement performed by ecocritical discourse itself (Kroeber 1).

As Kingsolver understands it, ecological knowledge works to dismantle inherited forms of domination, be it racial (in *Animal Dreams* and *The Lacuna*) or patriarchal (in *The Poisonwood Bible* and *Unsheltered*). In Kingsolver's fictional universe, ecology works to revivify perception and imagination; things in the world refract a changed image of how history and time can be understood differently. In a word, her landscape is animated and suffused with sites of becoming and soul-formation, an ecology convincingly described by Karen E.

Waldron as "[a] living model of both forming and dramatically changing relations to space and place, of multiple forming and changing systems of meaning and knowing, multiple forming and changing frames or ecologies, where both boundaries—for example, of the nation or continent, of ethnicity, river, or ocean—and movement across boundaries—of immigrants, flora and fauna, cultural practices, and pathogens—are necessary to understanding" (17). From the movement of immigrants and the question of their rights that Kingsolver encounters personally in the Sanctuary Movement to conceptualizing intersectional dimensions of place, her fiction constantly foregrounds how the human being and the environment depend upon each other—this dialectic prioritizes care over dominance, responsibility over neglect.

Material Ecocriticism and the Sentience of the World

An important contemporary thematic within ecocriticism can be defined as "materialistic," or returning critical attention to the ways in which inanimate matter speaks back to our embedded sense of environment. Theorists of material ecocriticism are concerned with illustrating the sentience of matter in terms of underscoring a fuller sense of human embodiment within an ever-changing ecosystem. Accordingly material ecocriticism emphasizes "the material interchanges across human bodies, animal bodies, and the wider material world," deconstructing the porous boundaries between the human and the nonhuman, raw matter and cultural mediation (Alaimo 476). The world talks back at us as a copartner in a narrative of becoming in which "there is no definitive break between sentient and nonsentient entities or between material and spiritual phenomena" (Coole and Frost 10). As we read Kingsolver's fiction, we will not only be conscious of how this interconnectedness becomes an underlying theme, but also of how the environment possesses an agential force that defines her characters' sense of identity and scope of ethical responsibility.

The prominent ecocritical theorist Wendy Wheeler enunciates a notion of "biosemiotics," where the ubiquity of signs in which "what is external and internal (whether things or ideas), both subjective and . . . objective, are treated by 'readers' (whether fungi, plants, nonhuman animals or human animals, cells and organelles, organs and body systems in generally) equally as *semiotic* objects" (21). In Wheeler's framework *all* matter understands and responds to stimuli in their own particular way—human intelligence is not the primary motor within the ecosystem. Kingsolver's characters are ethical readers of nature, learning to understand the ways in which nonhuman life reacts and responds to the decisions we make to change our ecosystem (whether it is logging a forest in *Flight Behavior* or hunting the keystone predator in *Prodigal*

Summer) and how the human "reader" is by that token changed by the unfolding ecological text. This dislodges the imperiousness of anthropocentric narrative, giving voice to the numerous, unrecorded stories that are being told by nonhuman figures. Their fragmented and multidimensional histories not only unsettle the human being's claim to centrality, but also testify to multiple scales of dynamic interaction that cuts across species and forms of life.

Material ecocriticism leverages the postmodern destabilization of the separation between the human realm and the natural environment to emphasize how much of "nature" is within us. The philosopher Jane Bennett has argued for a worldview wherein every organism is "inextricably enmeshed in a dense network of relations" (13). For Bennett, the undeniable agency of matter not only destroys the image of the human species as central and superior to the rest of nature, but also acknowledges the creativity of nonhuman species as they shape and change the environment. Bennett accordingly exhorts us to develop new modes of "perception that enable us to consult nonhumans more closely, or to listen and respond more carefully to their outbreaks, objections, testimonies, and propositions" (108). In Kingsolver's hands, narrative allows her readers to approach the fragile coexistence of human and nonhuman species with empathy and sentiment. This focus on sentimentality does not imply that Kingsolver resorts to a phony emotionalism that diminishes her work as pandering or nonartistic. Instead, Kingsolver's "sentimentalism seeks to redress isolation and detachment by exploring and emphasizing human connection through empathetic understanding" (Magee 66): *Flight Behavior* bears witness to the uncertain fate of the displaced monarch butterflies through Dellarobia's empathetic connection with them, a position that stresses the utter entanglement of human narrative with the narrative of dispossession, exile, and loss that the butterflies evince.

In the critical effort to "hear" as many narrative voices as possible, literary strategy becomes important to the work of material ecocriticism. As Serpil Oppermann writes, "the concept of narrative agency becomes paradigmatic to material ecocriticism, always instigating entangled relations that are often conflictual but always already rich with interpenetration of various beings, discourses, meanings, and materiality" (34). This utter interpenetration of the human with the nonhuman, rational with the material, coheres with what Heather Sullivan calls "dirt theory," a perspective that recognizes how "soil actively participates in small-scale ecological processes that are themselves integrated into the larger niches of other assemblages" (516). Accompanying Kingsolver's determined focus on the physicality of material processes is also the poetic perception that narrative can only ever be about rootedness within place, a heterotopic space that is both human and nonhuman, demarcated and open to flows and intersections.

Ecofeminism and the Gendered Difference of Kingsolver's Writing

Another strand of ecocritical theorizing relevant to Kingsolver's work is ecofeminism. In Kingsolver's declaiming of various injustices and instances of oppression that debar empathetic responses toward human and nonhuman others, patriarchal and anthropocentric dominance and exploitation articulate themselves in tandem. Ecofeminist critics focus on the unjustified equating of the category "nature" with "femininity" within patriarchal discourse, with the labeling of both as ideologically inferior and passive (thereby open to dominance) serving as justification for regimes of violence and despoilation. The philosopher Val Plumwood explains how systems of inequality are similarly premised upon this binary logic of exclusion and devaluation: "Racism, colonialism and sexism have drawn their conceptual strength from casting sexual, racial and ethnic difference as closer to the animal and the body construed as a sphere of inferiority, as a lesser form of humanity lacking the full measure of rationality or culture" (4). We might see Plumwood's commentary as being entirely relevant to Kingsolver's impassioned critique of colonialism in *The Poisonwood Bible*: the natural world and the feminine are positioned as mute and inadequate, dependent upon masculine authority because their meanings cannot be legitimized outside of patriarchal construction.

An ecofeminist critique challenges these assumptions on two fronts. First, this criticism allows the many forms of alienation and hierarchical domination present in heteronormative culture to be exposed and subjected to scrutiny. The linking of the feminine body and the environment allows critical discourse to articulate how "women experience the results of toxic dumping on their own bodies (sites of reproduction of the species), in their own homes (sites of the reproduction of daily life), and in their communities and schools (sites of social reproduction)" (Merchant 161). Patriarchy disavows its dependence on the feminine and the natural by repeating its acts of violence as normative practice. Kingsolver's novelistic logic of enmeshment performs this imbrication of the political with the social, demonstrating how patriarchal domination is an indelible part of history and the experience of daily life under capitalistic conditions. Her idealistic notion that human beings can refashion society to accommodate more ethical social practices cannot be divorced from her elegiac witnessing of the historical dimensions of cultural trauma, be it the forced dispossession of Native American land enacted by the American government in *The Bean Trees*, or the stripping away of civil liberties written into the Constitution in *The Lacuna*.

Second, an ecofeminist critique destabilizes gendered and ecological hierarchies by emphasizing a queered excess in the feminine/natural that reorientates sexual and environmental co-belonging. The maternal body then functions not as a secondary appendage to the masculine one, but as an impetus to rethink corporeal independence and fragility. As Jessica Benjamin notes, "the combination of resonance and difference that the mother offers can open the way to a recognition that transcends mastery and mechanical response, to a recognition that is based on *mutuality*" (35). Dominance cannot be ethically replaced by another schema of hierarchical subjugation—the feminine enacts an entirely different way of considering relationality. A fictional practice of mutuality, vulnerability, and codependence suitably informs the life-affirming nature of Kingsolver's novelistic vision, suffused throughout with chances and opportunities for renewal and redemption if only perspective is adjusted, vision clarified.

Kingsolver's fiction is filled with positive depictions of mutuality, usually fostered and nurtured by women. As Thera Wrede notes, Kingsolver "distinguishes a central impediment to male relationality in a cultural script that, expecting men to be independent, often thwarts their intersubjectivity. Conversely, emphasizing relationships, women's social role[s] facilitate relationality" (41). The impromptu, makeshift family that gathers around Taylor Greer in *The Bean Trees* and *Pigs in Heaven* emphasizes how familial ties transcend bloodlines to embrace a communal definition of care, responsibility, and mutual coexistence. These invite powerful reconsiderations of patriarchal definitions of kinship, inheritance, and generational ties. For Kingsolver nature provides an altered image of how social arrangements *could* be, locating the outlines of a utopian future within the everyday: rhizomatic plants in *The Bean Trees* and the matriarchy of coyote species in *Prodigal Summer* provide compelling metaphors for the naturalness of nonpatriarchal structures.

What Kingsolver ultimately demonstrates is how the ecofeminist position connects with political issues concerning justice and equity. If women have been systematically excluded from accessing cultural resources, the challenge is not to repeat this symbolic gesture by substituting "female" for "male," but to question essentialist constructs that establish clear conceptual boundaries. Kingsolver's fictional alternative is encapsulated by Marianne Hirsch as "an alternative to patriarchy and the logos, [which is] a world of shared female knowledge and experience in which subject/object dualism[s] and power relationships might be challenged and redefined" (133). For Kingsolver the ecofeminist stance turns disembodied consciousness toward the world as a *scene* of open-ended, interrelational evolving and becoming. For Rosi Braidotti ecocriticism invaluably intersects with the posthuman "turn" in the humanities through their common questioning of "the idea of a social order disconnected from its environmental and organic foundations and [the consequent] call for more complex schemes of understanding the multilayered form of interdependence between contemporary nature and culture" ("Critical Posthumanities" 385). In Kingsolver's passionate advocation of detailed attention to natural processes, and her invective against inegalitarian and unthinking cultural practices, her work speaks to the contemporary imagination in ways that renew conversations between scientists and literary scholars, policymakers, and the people on the ground. As we will see, literature matters in the world, as both rooted in reality and as a conceptual alternative to that reality.

Reading Kingsolver's Fictions with and beyond Theoretical Contexts

A comprehensive study of Kingsolver's fictions can further ecocritical discourse through her expressed adoption of literature as a medium that both entertains and instructs. For her, characters function as mouthpieces and examples through which she may enlighten the reader about relevant racial, political, and ecocritical themes she takes to be important to the ethical worldview she upholds and propagates. Writing resonates as "a fair enough vocation to strike one match after another against the dark isolation, when spectacular arrogance rules the day and tries to force hope into hiding" (*SW* 21). Kingsolver's aim is to imbue her reader with a utopian sense of hope that the world can be refashioned with the scientific and literary tools we currently have in hand that allow for a critical "examination of the stories that hold us together as a society and that we rely on to maintain our sense of identity" (*SW* 203). Kingsolver's determined belief in the inherent goodness and perfectibility of human society embodies an Enlightenment faith in scientific positivism and the tenets of humanism that may strike the critic immersed in much of the poststructuralist dimensions of ecocritical theory as overly essentialist.

However, her fiction responds through locating effective political and social intervention at the base level of practical human action. In other words, Kingsolver makes the abstractions of ecocritical theory *relatable* through fashioning characters from social milieus that her readers can identify with, combining emotional resonance with a clarion call to change specific aspects of their lives. Whereas ecocritical theory tends to subscribe to the "end" of the concept of the human as traditionally conceived by Western culture, Kingsolver brings back the importance of humanistic values of compassion and empathetic identification. This retrieval of positive interpersonal value opens new avenues of beneficial discourse that utilize scientific knowledge to aid us in making better decisions.

Second, Kingsolver's fiction espouses an indissoluble link between literature and life that eschews a contemporary postmodern questioning of literary representation. For Kingsolver real-world environmental crises such as climate degradation and unsustainable agricultural practices need to be represented in fiction as urgently and realistically as possible—her men and women of science do the much-needed work of combating ignorance and economic self-interest with rational discourse and careful attention to objective evidence. In this way Kingsolver is not so much interested in the theoretical wariness of construing knowledge about nature as a methodological construct as she is in investigating how situatedness within a contemporary climate of crisis challenges us to utilize the better aspects of human culture to forge more ethical ways of living. Indeed, Kingsolver's *Animal, Vegetable, Miracle* presents her family's practical experiment of sustainable consumption in rural Appalachia as a way to recalibrate existential relationships between the human being, land, and nonhuman agents. As she puts it, "in a nation pouring its resources into commodity agriculture—corn and soybeans everywhere and not a speck to eat—*back to the land* is an option with a permanent, quiet appeal" (*AVM* 179).

Reading Kingsolver's fiction through her moral vision is then not to subscribe to the view that her fiction resorts to an old-fashioned and outmoded literary style that shores up conventional pieties; it is to balance the theoretical perspectives of material ecocriticism with a practical look into the ways in which her best characters are able to combine knowledge with affective understanding, and idealism with pragmatism. For Kingsolver faithful representation of reality is akin to detailed attention to the world in all its terror and beauty. In a theoretical context, which can be too quick to turn away from "representation of nature" as a relic of pastoralism and religious pietism, Kingsolver accords significance to the power of the literary text to connect her readers to the very materiality out of which stories grow. In fact, paying attention is a form of devotion to the sense of place; as Kingsolver notes in her essay "The Memory Place," the pressing issue for any committed ecocritical perspective is how to "love the *imperfect* lands, the fragments of backyard desert paradise, the creek that runs between farms" (*HT* 180). Reading her fiction is thus to *ground* ourselves within her language, by seeing description as the literary materializing of an ethical stance—her novels are engaged in resolutely representing what is the case.

Holding the Line as the Entry Point to Kingsolver's Fictional Ethics

We may preface our analysis of Kingsolver's fictional work by drawing attention to her nonfiction book *Holding the Line: Women in the Great Arizona Mine Strike of 1983*, which was published in 1989, the year following *The Bean Trees*. In this account of the men and women who were part of the 1983–84 Phelps Dodge copper mine strike, Kingsolver blends her penchant for close observation with an idealistic outrage over the injustices committed by the powerful against the disenfranchised, themes that constantly accompany her later fiction. From listening to the many interviews she conducted with the men and women who were at the picket lines demanding "cost-of-living arrangements and medical benefits," Kingsolver understood how the power of resistance could become a fundamental principle (Wagner-Martin, *Barbara Kingsolver* 54). This informed her use of the fictional medium, a tool that presses back against the unethical complicity of governmental organization and capitalist agenda. As she states, writing the book "was a watershed event for me because it taught me to pay attention [and] to know the place where I lived" (*HL* xiv). Her fiction consequently is involved with politicizing the everyday, or to dramatize how her characters' sense of place is constantly changed and mediated by historical, economic, and political circumstances that raises the stakes for committed action against injustice and violence. Kingsolver's fiction is also given over to raising awareness about the disadvantaged and marginalized—people whose dignity has been diminished and brutalized by the very same governments elected to serve their needs. Observing the mining strike became formative for her because she "saw rights I'd taken for granted denied to people I'd learned to care about" (*HL* xiv).

Covering the strike also made her more sensitive toward issues of representation and how to use her fictional perspective in ways that challenge stereotypes and would inculcate respect for the Other. As Wagner-Martin details, the enforcement forces played on racial fault lines among the strikers by treating Hispanic people and women more harshly (*Barbara Kingsolver* 55). As she reflects on the strike, Kingsolver gloomily sounds the note of betrayal: "in a place a few hours drive from where I live, the government, the police, and a mining company formed a conspicuous partnership to break the lives of the people standing together for what they thought was right" (*HL* xxii). As we will see, the events of the strike find both direct and indirect expression in her fiction: *Animal Dreams* is "specifically placed in a mining town where people grow peaches, mix their metaphors, celebrate el Dia de los Muertos, and have to contend with a mining company that pollutes their groundwater with sulfuric acid—all of which I learned about from direct experience while following the Phelps Dodge strike" (*HL* xiv), while the economic plight of communities destroyed by inequitable economic policies is movingly rendered in novels such as *Flight Behavior* and *Demon Copperhead*.

What writing *Holding the Line* showed Kingsolver was "the power the story of injustice could have if it were properly presented," and we can understand her fiction as a space where the objectivity of a scientist, the impassioned rhetoric of an idealist, and the careful craft of a literary artist all meet and find dynamic expression (Wagner-Martin, *Barbara Kingsolver* 59). For Kingsolver "the lessons of class struggle and the survival value of collective action" are not so much abstract theoretical speculations as they are driven by real-world narratives of desperation and hope (*HL* xix). The value of approaching Kingsolver's work from an ecocritical perspective is not just that it spotlights her abiding concern for issues surrounding environmental justice. Ecocritical theory's prompting to reconceive the very bases of personhood and sociality cuts through political and economic logic, with a hope that life can be resumed under less oppressive existential conditions. What lessons Kingsolver finds in *Holding the Line* can be applied to the rest of her fiction. On the one hand, the book is "a cautionary tale" that warns us against trusting the very people who become more invested in looking after their economic interests instead of enacting policies geared toward meliorating inequality and injustice (*HL* xxiii). From her indictment of America's political involvement in postcolonial Africa as seen in *The Poisonwood Bible* to her more contemporary castigation of society's benighted attitude toward Darwinian evolution in *Unsheltered,* Kingsolver uses the historical perspective to warn us that freedom from political and intellectual oppression, and the individual right to expression, are fragile ideals that must be won again and again by acts of resistance and group solidarity. On the other hand, *Holding the Line* is a story about hope, a narrative of how the strikers "could bear the meanness of their nation without becoming mean-spirited themselves [and] could come away with passion for justice instead of revenge," and this image of humanity holds true throughout her fiction (*HL* xxiii).

Kingsolver's optimism emerges all the more strongly because she does not turn a blind eye toward hard-hitting issues such as rural poverty, domestic violence, sexual violation, and substance addiction—these stymie the human potential for change and signal desperately that life as it is lived must be reconceived under a different politics. However, Kingsolver's firm belief, as translated into her characters' bids for redemption, is that human beings are motivated to pursue goodness for themselves and for others. As this book will emphasize, Kingsolver's art is suffused by an idealism that offers healing in the aftermath of trauma and new possibilities from out the deadlock of advanced capitalist modernity. It is in her work that we see the efficacy of human action in transforming what meanings our contemporary situation will have in the face of a radically unpredictable future.

The Structure of This Book

This book offers a critical survey of the entire range of Kingsolver's novels, providing the reader with philosophical perspectives through which to understand the importance of difference in her work. For Kingsolver reinventing our relationship to the food we consume or toward the moral responsibilities we owe toward nonhuman species allows us to (re)turn toward ourselves in a fuller, more perceptive fashion. She signals that this reinvention is the antithesis of exploitative domination through her continual concern with encountering otherness. Kingsolver thus insists that negotiation with otherness through sharing and nonviolent abiding is the key for redefining the relationship between the self, history, and place. Kingsolver foregrounds fiction's ability to forge utopian imaginative spaces, a perspective that combines scientific attention to reality with the imaginative possibilities opened up by literary representation. By examining the working out of difference as it transpires in Kingsolver's commitment to dialogicity as it structures inquiry into history and the natural world, I point out a constant thrust in the fiction toward recalibration and reimagined ownership, both toward the individual and the community.

Chapter 2 will focus on Kingsolver's early novels *The Bean Trees* and *Pigs in Heaven* as part of an integrated narrative arc involving Taylor Greer, a young white woman who is suddenly entrusted with the responsibility of caring for a Native American infant. The chapter explores Taylor's feminine *Bildungsroman* in terms of her growth into maturity and self-understanding as a result of negotiating the borderlines between family and community, law and individual responsibility. I analyze the dialectics of self and otherness woven throughout the meeting-points between individuals, cultures, and communities to emphasize how the reader grows into insight along with Taylor by tapping on alternative patterns of belonging to the world outside of heteronormative definitions of kinship and bloodline. Kingsolver's interest in acknowledging the claims of alternative accounts of tradition on our historical situatedness emphasizes the embeddedness of the individual within larger patterns of meaning, which first need to be defamiliarized as prelude to an enlarged notion of worldhood and subjectivity.

Chapter 3 will focus on the presentation of female subjectivity and gender dynamics in Kingsolver's novels *Animal Dreams* and *The Poisonwood Bible*. It will explore the aesthetic dimensions of her use of the female voice and the "fractured" narrative as literary devices that render the (after)effects of trauma on the female psyche. Kingsolver's feminist strategy proceeds by showing how openness and vulnerability enable the self to process and transform trauma in ways that are denied to masculine modes of repression and incomplete sublimation. By comparing the use of the female narrators across these two novels, I argue that Kingsolver adumbrates a poetics of gendered "receptivity" that mitigates the obtuse imposition of a single ideological viewpoint. Acknowledging embeddedness allows one to recognize how one has been shaped by their past experiences. In the same gesture, these voices point toward an affective understanding of pain that maintains the necessary difficulties of living with, and growing out of, trauma. Self-understanding is thus once again tested through the struggle to maintain independence from the controlling aegis of the male voice, but Kingsolver suggests that her female voices receive otherness to the same extent that they are able to refashion a sense of self through this exchange, thereby being more able to respond ethically to the burden of historical guilt.

Chapter 4 will emphasize how Kingsolver pursues some of the major themes of ecocriticism and ecofeminism explicitly in the novels *Prodigal Summer* and *Flight Behavior*. By eschewing the drama of individuality to present the intertwining between the human being and his or her environment, Kingsolver implies how this enmeshment of the human being within a "whole system" once again gives rise to new possibilities of self-understanding. She dialecticizes the relationship between human and nonhuman communities by charting the intellectual and spiritual awakening of the characters in these novels, whose putative grasps at personal freedom and erstwhile narrow focuses on self-contained economic practices cedes to a widened understanding of the fragility of belonging to a world at once resilient and threatened by irreversible damage. Their moral "awakenings" become even more pressing given the catastrophic consequences of exploitation and the continuance of capitalist extraction. In this way the recovery of self, and the restoration of environmental justice for those who cannot speak or participate in language, cannot be separated from modes of relationality that go beyond the anthropocentric.

Chapter 5 sheds light on Kingsolver's turn toward historical fiction in the novels *The Lacuna* and *Unsheltered* and on her practice of feminist historiography, which works to celebrate the un-commemorated legacies and gaps silenced by heteronormative accounts of the past. By highlighting the lacuna in historical (re)construction, which is self-consciously filtered through present-day understanding, Kingsolver blasts open the historical record to interrogate the ways historical narratives need to give voice to indeterminacies and the possibilities of reading and understanding the past differently. Kingsolver problematizes the image of the past so that the understanding of intellectual tradition can be reactivated. This hermeneutical perspective enlists the imaginative capacity of literary language to uncover modes of recovery and rehabilitation that allow silent voices to emerge and alternative accounts of the past to be told.

Chapter 6 will analyze Kingsolver's most recent novel *Demon Copperhead* as an intertextual rewriting of Charles Dickens's *David Copperfield*. I focus on the novel's unsparing depiction of poverty and addiction, drawing a crucial metaphorical linkage between substance dependence and the inability to escape from a totalizing system of exploitation and degradation. Apart from her use of the form of the *Bildungsroman* as a narrative device like she did in *The Bean Trees* and *Pigs in Heaven*, this latest work from Kingsolver employs the same brand of observation and idealism that she espouses in her other novels to chart struggle and triumph in the face of dehumanization and the commodification of human bodies and experiences. As common themes emerge in this book's reading of the entire range of Kingsolver's novelistic output, we note her very simple, but profound, artistic attempt to reclaim different narratives about our belonging to the world that would otherwise be silenced or marginalized.

CHAPTER 2

Release, Gathering, and Responsibility
The Bean Trees and *Pigs in Heaven*

Kingsolver's early novels *The Bean Trees* (published 1988) and *Pigs in Heaven* (published 1993) center around the coming-of-age story of Taylor Greer, a disaffected young white woman whose life changes with the sudden assumption of maternal responsibility for an abandoned Native American child she names Turtle. Having the baby abruptly thrust into her hands in a diner she stops by on her road trip away from the suffocating conditions of her domicile, the reader's interest in these two novels is sustained by Taylor's coming to terms with the need for groundedness and a renewed understanding of community as part of her care for Turtle's well-being and safety. More broadly conceived, Kingsolver's narrative concerning the abandonment, adoption, and reintegration of the young child Turtle asks the reader to reimagine the fundamental bases of ownership and belonging as a prelude to reimagining our relationality to the places we call home and to the people we call family. Her extended treatment of the bonds of maternal responsibility, care, and accountability formed between Turtle and Taylor Greer loosens conventional markers of sociality and identity, giving voice to larger, more diffuse ways of locating the individual within a community. Kingsolver is adamant that embracing diversity and difference entails a more positive way of conceptualizing our collective interdependence than the white, capitalist ideology of sufficient individuality. In an interview with Stephen L. Fisher, Kingsolver states that "it does strike me that our great American mythology tends to celebrate separate achievement and separateness when in fact nobody does anything alone" (27).

The recognition of our shared fragility thereby engenders an alternative epistemology, which may be called ecocritical, wherein rapacious consumption and exploitation is replaced with dogged care for objects and people entrusted to us, and responsibility is attuned toward restoring the relationship between the individual and his or her community. Kingsolver's early attunement toward ecofeminism is made apparent, wherein the self-sacrificial nature of the women surrounding Taylor allows the reader to imagine care and nurturance in ways that transcend the traditional bourgeois ideal of the nuclear family. Indeed, Taylor's awakening from disaffection into the possibilities of redefinition are matched onto her appreciation of the fecundity of natural growth—observing her surroundings, she remarks that she "just couldn't imagine where all this life was coming from," (*BT* 119) and that paying attention to nature "made you sense the world differently" (*BT* 135). As we will see later, nature for Kingsolver is not a mute canvass her characters impose their desires upon; instead, natural images provide a compelling metaphor through which to redescribe human fraternity and belonging. In short the ecocritical perspective decenters anthropocentric ways of knowledge in favor of an imbrication between the human and the nonhuman.

Jeanette E. Riley, Kathleen M. Torrens, and Susan T. Krumholz emphasize the ecofeminist aspects of Kingsolver's novelistic vision, and how it describes a nonpatriarchal notion of social justice in which the "collective accountability, empathy, connection, community, and active participation in a world around us" become important acculturated moral responses to historical and environmental crises (105). As I will demonstrate in my analysis of *The Bean Trees* and *Pigs in Heaven*, this response motivates redressal of past wrongs by instituting more egalitarian modes of social organizations that blend the improvisational with the codified. Taylor's personal spiritual growth in these two novels is thus underpinned both by her fearsome determination to eke out a shared existence for herself and Turtle, despite her own inexperience concerning motherhood, and the inevitable limitations of that ethic of care when balanced against the support and nurture that an entire community can provide to meet Turtle's developmental needs.

Kingsolver's arguable idealization of the Cherokee Nation as utopic space for Turtle's future beyond the pages of the narrative is tempered by her evocation of the unresolvable trauma that links Turtle's personal history to the institutionalized deracination of the Native American population by the U.S. government. As Taylor's mother Alice Greer comments about the violence inflicted upon the Cherokees by nonindigenous settlers, "it's monstrous, what one person will do to another" (*PH* 282), echoing her daughter's earlier lament that "this world was a terrible place to try to bring up a child in" (*BT* 185). Reading *The Bean Trees* and *Pigs in Heaven* as an extended narrative about loss and recovery highlights Kingsolver's politics of community and ecological responsibility as transformative counterimages of restoration that challenge deep-seated notions of class and racial belonging. In other words Kingsolver acknowledges the multiple sources of inequality that lie at the heart of a normative definition of culture without suggesting that these divisive frameworks are ineradicable.

As Heather Houser comments, Kingsolver's imbrication of Taylor's mini-*Bildungsroman* with the process of healing that the Cherokee community undertakes to right its wrongs by claiming Turtle as one of their own echoes "a historical conception . . . experienced as loss and an emergent manifestation as a site of activism and knowledge production opening unto hope" (109). In terms of the overall argument of this book, this "production of knowledge" as utopic praxis cannot be separated from the creative potentialities of difference that allow us to view the world from a changed perspective. It is this positive reimagining that forms the basis of Magali Cornier Michael's detailed study of Kingsolver's two novels. For Michael, Kingsolver "reconfigure[s] the individual as inextricable from the community and vice-versa, which in turn allows for new conceptions of community, family, and agency" (110). The claims of ownership over property, genealogy, and place are deactivated in favor of a fluidity forged and continued by voluntary connections and existential exigencies. In Kingsolver's paradoxical formulation, it is in the recognition and negotiation of difference that a practice of "embeddedness" and belonging is possible in the first place (*AVM* 334).

The intellectual and cultural boundaries separating the human being from the natural world, and white from non-white, need to be broken down. This is not to resort to a facile universalism that obliterates the specificity of the lived perspective of the other, but to articulate communal resources for living a fuller, more responsible existence through the acknowledgment of the difference of the other. Kingsolver's moral vision is thereby antithetical to reductiveness and imperious exclusivity; for her, "successful partnerships between people and their habitats" define much-needed attitudes of collaboration, conservation, and mutual responsibility (*AVM* 77). As *The Bean Trees* demonstrates, by practicing practical modes of altruism, tied to the specific needs and demands of the other, the female characters try to "make things as right as [they] can" (*BT* 233). Kingsolver's feminism is not necessarily co-opted into a reactionary stance against patriarchal dominance but is oriented toward how these characters "take the lead in establishing healthier ecologies, along the way working to overcome the retrograde tendencies of their male mates or associates" (Bender 126). In my analysis of Kingsolver's first novel, I aim to trace and follow this makeshift, collaborationist feminist community that supplies a healing corrective against masculine public institutions that fail the most vulnerable members of society, as indexed through Turtle and the Guatemalan refugees Estevan and Esperanza. The chance encounters between these characters afford Kingsolver the opportunity to dramatize the *happening* of community and family defined not so much through genealogy and bloodline as through camaraderie and shared responsibility. In this way the reader confronts and acknowledges difference as positive counterimage to the status quo, enlivening his or her relationship to personal and collective history.

Ownership, Responsibility, and Community in *The Bean Trees*

Kingsolver's protagonist Taylor Greer emerges from this novel as a character who combines the stereotypically masculine traits of tenacity and insouciant vigor with the feminine characteristics of nurturance and conviviality. Her personal mobility as she travels from Kentucky to Arizona before ending up in Oklahoma not only resonates with the popular genre of the road-trip narrative, but also echoes mythical stories of exile and travel. For Catherine Himmelwright, this desire for adventure and self-definition on Taylor's part results in a novel forging of the Western male archetypical figure of the solo traveler with the feminine enactment of maternal care, when a helpless Turtle is put into her hands: "Barbara Kingsolver finds a way to unite the possibilities of a garden with the opportunities for adventure in *The Bean Trees*, her novel about a woman's migration from the American South to the American West. Merging these characteristics: the desire for movement and the desire to tend to a home, Kingsolver is able to express a female voice that has heretofore been lost or subsumed by the white male experience. . . . By combining these two figures, Kingsolver fashions a new American mythology that unites both male and female imaginative constructions" (120).

This dialectic between the adolescent bid for autonomy and hearkening to the larger forces of community that precede the individual defines the early sections of the novel, framing Taylor's road-trip not as an escape from the constricting forces of family and place, but as a necessary detour en route to a discovery of the healing potentialities of relationality and rootedness within a community. Kingsolver's drama of loss and recovery is foreshadowed in Taylor's musing about her name as she starts her trip away from Pittman County, Kentucky. Along with the sense of her newfound freedom comes the idea that she "would get [herself] a new name" so as to "make a clean break" (*BT* 12). This desire for self-definition through forging a new identity is immediately counteracted by the thought that "a name is not something a person really has the right to pick out, but is something you're provided with more or less by chance" (*BT* 12). This focus on provision and contingency not only modulates the masculine illusion of an individual self completely determined by his choices and desires, but also underlines the thematic of connectivity to previous generations as indexed through the bestowal of a name. Kingsolver thereby reflects the importance of naming as linguistic conflux between the human being and his or her environment in the specificity of her Cherokee characters like Annawake Fourkiller and Cash Stillwater, undercutting any notion of permanent ownership over individual circumstance to negate the responsibility we owe toward other members of our community who have been entrusted into our care.

Kingsolver's focus on an expanded notion of care and responsibility, and the positive effects of nurturance, finds crucial expression in the "adoption" scene involving Taylor's impromptu assumption of the role of mother and caregiver to Turtle. This scene emphasizes the confusion, fear, and reluctance Taylor displays toward this chance bestowal of another human being, who is by definition nameless and stateless, into her care:

> "Look," I said, "even if you wanted to, you can't just give somebody a kid. You have to have the papers and stuff. Even a car has papers, to prove you didn't steal it."
>
> "This baby has no papers. There isn't nobody knows it's alive, or cares. Nobody that matters, like the police or nothing like that. This baby was born in a Plymouth."
>
> "Well, it didn't happen this morning," I said. "Plymouth or no Plymouth, this child has been around long enough for somebody to notice." I has a foggy understanding that I wasn't arguing the right point. This was getting us nowhere.
>
> [Taylor] put her hands where the child's shoulders might be, under all that blanket, and pushed it gently back into the seat, trying to make it belong there. She looked at it for a long time. Then she closed the door and walked away. (*BT* 19)

Focalizing the scene through Taylor's perspective, Kingsolver allows the reader to not only feel the utter randomness of this negligent assignation on the unknown woman's part, but also to empathize with Taylor's understanding that this is a burden she is obligated to bear, despite having no prior connections to Turtle. As Linda Wagner-Martin aptly points out, we are compelled to participate in Taylor's narrative in part due to her "recognizable fear of the huge undertaking of being a parent" (*Barbara Kingsolver's World* 27). As Taylor struggles to accommodate her need for personal freedom with small, practical actions undertaken for the sake of the vulnerable child placed in her charge, Kingsolver emphasizes how Taylor gradually grows into maturity as she steps into her role as provider and defender of Turtle.

In this way Kingsolver rescripts the literary genre of the *Bildungsroman* by suggesting how the female protagonist's achievement of moral insight concomitant with the assumption of a vocation is not so much conveyed via a struggle between herself and her environment, but through the attainment of a more profound sense of interpersonal relationality mapped onto natural processes of growth, nurture, and bearing fruit—a thematic resonance also borne out in Kingsolver's narratives of personal and artistic growth in *The Lacuna* and *Demon Copperhead*. As Himmelwright points out, "rather than relying on the power of the individual and the individual's ability to conquer challenges on his own, Kingsolver creates a female character who is empowered and able to transform herself and others through the act of creation" (134). This deemphasis of individuality once again enlarges the concept of responsibility and accountability, not so much for the consequences accrued due to acts resulting from personal volition, but for all living beings placed in our care (whom we owe a duty toward). Indeed, Kingsolver marries social responsibility with ecological consciousness in Taylor's description of Turtle's "attach[ing] itself to me by its little hands like roots sucking on dry dirt," the simile implying a productive similarity-in-dissimilarity between the human and natural world (*BT* 22). By using literary language to forge synergies between these two spheres while resisting collapsing and conflating natural and social processes, Kingsolver enlists difference as a way of allowing us to perceive the world as *another*. This perception decenters the anthropocentric drive toward mastery and dominance in favor of highlighting the urgent need to care and share the burden of caring that is necessary for life to flourish. Emphasizing the interpersonal over the solipsistic thereby engenders a deeper embeddedness within a healthier ecology of interconnectedness and communal dependence.

Kingsolver's reimagining of community in the novel takes its focus from the creative potentialities of women who band together in a rough-and-ready fashion. As Wagner-Martin points out, Kingsolver's investment in mythology in this context draws from "a set of ancient matriarchal myths about the female power to engender" (*Barbara Kingsolver's World* 26). Kingsolver provides a counterpoint to Taylor's narrative through the story of Lou Ann Ruiz, an Arizonian woman who has to raise her son Dwayne Ray on her own after her disabled husband leaves her. After Lou Ann takes Taylor in as an informal boarder, the two characters naturally draw close to each other. Kingsolver paints a lively picture of a supportive female network of single mothers who sacrifice energy and material resources for each other as part of what Kingsolver calls "compassionate local actions," which eschew abstract humanitarian clichés for practical acts of kindness (*AVM* 150). Taylor is herself taken aback by Lou Ann's altruism, going so far as to comment that "it's not like we're a *family*, for Christ's sake. You've got your own life to live, and I've got mine. You don't have to do all this stuff for me" (*BT* 89). Insofar as Taylor's definition of family is still bounded and defined by the patriarchal unit, she misses Kingsolver's larger point about rethinking community and belonging outside of the nuclear structure that has been foisted upon society by political and cultural systems that systematically disadvantage women such as herself. As Michael comments, "*The Bean Trees* challenges the 'cultural image of family in the United States . . . of a heterosexual couple, their offspring, and relatives by blood or marriage' that continues to dominate despite the 'variety of family forms' that characterize American culture at the turn of the twenty-first century" (87).

Taylor's informal "adoption" of Turtle is thereby a microcosmic reflection of the positive, ad-hoc nature of the "extended family" that gathers around Lou Ann: Taylor, Turtle, Mattie (the owner of the tire shop Taylor works in), and the Guatemalan couple Estevan and Esperanza. As Kingsolver reiterates, the ties of responsibility the members of this community owe to one another derive not from bloodlines, but from reciprocal generosity. The novel's forging of alternative modes of kinship can again be seen as part of Kingsolver's questioning of ownership and exclusionist modes of thought: if the cultural hegemony of the patriarchal familial unit, along with its traditional control over property, wealth, and resources, can be destabilized, then nonhierarchical ways of encountering and preserving life are worthy of consideration and practice. By returning a different image of what is conventional, or by defamiliarizing entrenched societal structures, Kingsolver maintains her interest in transforming these norms in the service of utopic existential alternatives.

That Kingsolver offers this alternative does not mean that she indulges in an escapist fantasy. On the contrary, the novel is very much aware of the ways American society has failed its most vulnerable members. This harshness is forcefully reflected on Turtle's body in "bruises and worse" indicating sexual abuse; more indirectly, the neglect by her birthparents results in her inability to flourish (*BT* 23). It is thus telling that Kingsolver has the doctor Taylor visits comments about the toddler's "physical and emotional deprivation" that disallows her to continue "growing," the use of an ecological metaphor further emphasizing the vital links between the human organism and his or her environment (*BT* 129). Kingsolver thereby pursues a definition of the human individual as indelibly shaped by the community he or she participates in and is nurtured by—the idea of the solitary ego is anathema to her moral vision. In this respect the literary allusion to *Silas Marner* proves to be apposite to the novel, for both Taylor and the lonely protagonist of George Eliot's novel take on the responsibility of raising a child, who in turn plays an instrumental role in rejuvenating their caregiver's relationship to his or her community (*BT* 185).

Eliot's positive portrayal of organic social ties in a rural setting similarly reflects some of Kingsolver's themes: the interconnectedness between people, the benefits of meliorative efforts to restore interpersonal bonds, and the indissoluble link between the human being and his or her environment. It therefore becomes all the more pressing to remediate Turtle's traumatic past by placing her within a different sort of community, one which is defined by an ethos of sharing:

> "Now," [Estevan] went on, "you can go and visit heaven. What? You see a room just like the first one, the same table, the same pot of stew, the same spoons as long as a sponge mop. But these people are all happy and fat."
>
> "Real fat, or do you mean just well-fed?" Lou Ann asked.
>
> "Just well-fed," he said. "Perfectly, magnificently well-fed, and very happy. Why do you think?"
>
> He pinched up a chunk of pineapple in his chopsticks, neat as you please, and reached all the way across the table to offer it to Turtle. She took it like a newborn bird. (*BT* 113)

It is no coincidence that Turtle's first words, after not being able to speak for a long time, "ran to vegetables," for her language bears fruit in the same way that her new life flourishes within this utopic space of possibility (*BT* 105). It is also this embeddedness within her alternate community that allows Taylor, and the reader, to reflect more deeply about the sense of home and relationships between the self and the other. These ideas will come together in the tragic story of Estevan and Esperanza, preparing the way for Taylor's struggle of defining "home" for Turtle when the basis of her claim on the child is challenged by Annawake from the Cherokee tribe.

Home, the Loss of a World, and Recovery in the Drama of Adoption

Kingsolver's attempt to reimagine the ethical nature of community takes on clearest expression in the novel through the story of Estevan and Esperanza. Through their story, she tackles the issue of rights for migrants who have been denied a home and a cultural history due to political oppression. For Kingsolver, the importance of interconnectedness and embeddedness within a human community means that the responsibilities that we owe to one another transcend national boundaries and political interests, precipitating themselves through daily, practical actions that change the conditions of existence for the vulnerable other. Kingsolver's critique of public institutions that fail those most in need here extends beyond the individual story of Turtle to encompass the multitude of unnamed Central American refugees whose basic human dignity has been denied them. Mattie tells Taylor a story "about a migrant lemon picker in Phoenix who lost a thumb in a machine and bled to death because the nearest hospital turned him away" (*BT* 137). As discussed earlier, Kingsolver does not shy away from depicting human cruelty and neglect alongside a more utopic portrayal of redemption: part of Taylor's growth is her coming to understand that human beings are forced by circumstances and exigencies to compromise themselves.

Indeed, meeting Estevan and Esperanza and learning about their tragic backgrounds provide a crucial opportunity for her to contextualize Turtle's abandonment within a wider debilitating ecology of moral dilemma and the failure of politics. Estevan and Esperanza's child Ismene "was taken in a raid on their neighborhood" by government forces who suspect Estevan of sedition because of his profession as an English teacher in Guatemala (*BT* 142). Because they refuse to surrender the names of the other seventeen members of the teachers' union, Ismene is forever lost to them. This act of violence and naked show of power implicitly links the narratives of Estevan and Esperanza, Turtle's biological mother, and Annawake (whose twin brother was also forcefully taken away from her family) through these characters' struggles with the trauma of losing or surrendering a family member due to forces outside of their control. Taylor's personal horror at a world "where people have to make choices like that" is the catalyst to her looking outside her erstwhile narrow definitions of choice, autonomy, and individual freedom, thereby allowing her to recognize how her decisions for Turtle's well-being fit into a larger pattern of restoration and ecological melioration (*BT* 143).

If Kingsolver's implicit intertextual reference to *Silas Marner* allows her novel to reflect some of the more positive presentations of community in the Victorian novel, then her explicit reference to Sophocles's play *Antigone*—through the name Ismene—demonstrates a negative counterimage to Eliot's idea of inclusion and social harmony. As Marianne Novy details, "in Sophocles, Ismene was the traditionally submissive woman who rebuked her sister for her daring. If Kingsolver's Ismene, the missing child, adopted into a prosperous fascist family apparently without knowledge of her past, is comparable to Sophocles' Ismene . . . [then] Antigone is the prototype of the characters in the novel involved in the sanctuary movement, who are committing civil disobedience to protect refugees persecuted in their own country" (194). This disobedience defines an ethics of hospitality and responsibility for the other at positive variance from prevailing political norms, decentering the notion of community and family away from artificial markers of citizenship and filiation toward an *othered* image of home in the widest, and most humane, sense. This humanity is duly voiced by Mattie, who affirms that "we have a legal obligation to take in people whose lives are in danger" (*BT* 108). Kingsolver ironically juxtaposes

Mattie's hospitality to the empty claims of political rhetoric as conveyed by Emma Lazarus's poem "The New Colossus" (published 1883): the words of the sonnet celebrating the unlimited welcoming of the "tired" and "poor" to America are powerfully undercut by the harshness of treatment faced by refugees like Estevan and Esperanza (*BT* 237).

Just as *Antigone* champions the private claims of the individual over and against the monolithic power of the ruler of the *polis*, Kingsolver's sympathy is with the characters who are forced out of the state and marked by a total exclusion from political participation and rights. Indeed, Kingsolver demands that her reader recognize the ugly reality behind America's triumphalist mythology of success in its failure to properly come to terms with the history of oppression and violence perpetuated on native populations. Through Estevan's sharing with Taylor, Kingsolver maps the destruction of "whole villages of [Mayan] Indians" with the forced relocation of the Cherokee people outside of their indigenous settlements (*BT* 205). Kingsolver's focus on loss extends beyond the familial to include the vanishing of an entire world and way of knowing for Estevan's people: the destruction of language and culture lends to an irresolvable trauma of "not belonging in any place" (*BT* 205). Kingsolver's engagement with this history of loss, deracination, and relocation is her way of using the power of literary fiction to speak against issues such as racism and immigrant rights. This rightly demands a creative rethinking of relationality and political community, whose positive image in her early fiction is to be sought in the "rich, lively, symbiotic, interconnected community of women" that forms the ideal analogue to ecological co-belonging and interdependence (Beattie 160). It is therefore no coincidence that Taylor reflects how "more often than not . . . the woman carried the man through the tragedy" in variance to the stereotypical image of the masculine hero saving the helpless woman from peril (*BT* 192). What Kingsolver offers to replace the various essentialisms that separate people from one another is "the need for a hybrid society favouring feminism and tribal forms of community over the lone masculine individualist" (Cohen 147).

For Kingsolver adoption happily reconciles the active assumption of responsibility over another person's well-being (along with the chance for healthy reintegration into a larger collective) with the recognition that this responsibility does not betoken possessive ownership. As Novy points out, Taylor's faux adoption of Turtle represents the ideal balance between the latter's bloodline and the maternal bonds assumed by the former, forging "a comfortable hybrid identity in which both nurture and heredity are recognized" (197). However, this resolution of identity is balanced by Taylor's growing acknowledgment that she will have to surrender some degree of ownership over her child, foreshadowing Turtle's eventual assimilation into the Cherokee Nation, which forms the natural conclusion of Taylor's narrative. Signs of this recognition play out first in the closing pages of *The Bean Trees*, where Taylor is "bothered" by how "Turtle was calling Esperanza 'Ma'," her resentment underlined by the fact that she can never fully lay claim to Turtle (*BT* 201). Despite the deceit perpetuated by Estevan, Esperanza, and Taylor at the local adoption office that Turtle is a child being given up by her Cherokee birth parents Estevan and Esperanza, this gesture brings some measure of comfort to Esperanza. As Estevan remarks, everything happens *as if* Esperanza were giving up Ismene for adoption, thereby finding "a safe place to leave Ismene behind" (*BT* 233). Kingsolver here acknowledges the power that a fictional drama of adoption has to heal the trauma of separation. It is therefore the momentary belief in a story that allows "the creation of plausible if not verifiable narratives" to forge a therapeutic relationality with the past (Homans 7). By linking Turtle with Ismene and connecting Esperanza's past with the future that Taylor forges with her child, Kingsolver once again highlights how the cultural resources afforded by the alternative community she has depicted in the novel go a significant way to restoring the larger injustices and imbalances inflicted upon the vulnerable members of the community by historical circumstances.

Kingsolver's final image of this nurturing interconnectedness turns upon the wisteria vine and its system of roots, which form a perfect ecosystem. If the metaphor strikes the reader as being direct to a fault, it resonates with the novel's deliberate arrangement and manipulation of events to achieve its happy ending:

> But this is the most interesting part: wisteria vines, like other legumes, often thrive in poor soil, the book said. Their secret is something called rhizobia. These are microscopic bugs that live underground like little knots on the roots. They suck nitrogen gas right out of the soil and turn it into fertilizer for the plant.
>
> The rhizobia are not actually part of the plant, they are separate creatures, but they always live with legumes: a kind of underground railroad moving secretly up and down the roots.
>
> "It's like this," I told Turtle. "There's a whole invisible system for helping out the plant you'd never guess was there." (*BT* 241)

This resolution has been called into question by readers unhappy with Kingsolver's seeming complicity with the historical removal of an Indian child from her habitat by a white person. As Margaret Homans points out, "the entire plot of abandonment, adoption, search and reunion is propelled not by allegiance to historical truth but by the narrative requirements of the white female protagonist" (19). In a narrative driven by Taylor's need to decide "what's best for

Turtle," Kingsolver neglects to consider the perspectives of the Cherokee people and their own definitions of kinship, community, and familial ties (*PH* 341).

To be fair Kingsolver herself has acknowledged the representational limits and difficulties which stem from her artistic decisions in *The Bean Trees*. As she remarks, "I realized with embarrassment that I had completely neglected a moral area when I wrote about this Native American kid being swept off the reservation and raised by a loving white mother. It was something I hadn't thought about, and I felt I needed to make that right in another book" (Perry 165). *Pigs in Heaven* readjusts this inadvertent bias through a presentation of difference as structuring motif. As we will see, Kingsolver builds in tension through the difference between Western and non-Western ways of knowing, with the explicit aim of inculcating a respect and legitimacy for Native American society with their "own government" and social and cultural norms (*BT* 213). It is thus in the struggle between Taylor and Annawake in the later novel that the reader is forced to adjudicate between ethical claims that, as Kingsolver positions them, have equal weight and urgency.

Competing Claims and the Struggle for Legitimacy in *Pigs in Heaven*

Kingsolver's extension and resolution of Taylor's narrative sees her giving more attention to the difference between "western, nuclear families and tribal, extended families" in the struggle between Taylor and Annawake Fourkiller, a young and fiercely intelligent Cherokee lawyer who investigates the legality of Turtle's adoption (Schultermandl 226). For Annawake, Taylor's Cherokee heritage is the paramount reason Turtle should be assimilated back into Cherokee society, and Annawake holds on to this reason firmly in her conversations with Taylor and Alice Greer, Taylor's mother. In order to allow her reader to shift away from an exclusive focus on Taylor's determination to hold on to Turtle (a position that we have come to empathize with during the course of *The Bean Trees*), Kingsolver shifts to a third-person narratorial voice that uses free indirect discourse to allow flexibility in rendering the thoughts and feelings of multiple characters. This shift allows us entry into the very personal reasons why Annawake is determined to challenge Taylor and her family over Turtle's birthright.

In this way the reader comes to understand the magnitude of Annawake's psychological wounding because of the forced removal of her brother Gabe from her family due to racist government policies against the Native American population—she feels his disappearance as deeply as a "stitch in her side . . . [in] the place where they tore him out" (*PH* 60). As Annawake elaborates in a series of debates between herself and Alice, "our chain of caretaking got interrupted" when the Native American children were relocated (*PH* 227). The historical circumstances surrounding this official policy of relocation and removal is elaborated upon by legal scholar Sarah Sargent as such:

> For several decades, the United States government pursued a policy of removing American Indian children from their families and communities. The removal was in various guises. One was the use of off-reservation boarding schools. Another was the placement of children for adoption in white, non-American Indian homes. These removal tactics were designed to break the ties that the children had to their identity as American Indians, and to their language, culture and religion. . . . One example of this is the Indian Adoption Project run by the Child Welfare League of America, which viewed placement of children away from their tribal communities as advantageous for the child. (51–52)

For Annawake what is at stake is the loss of cultural memory because of the adoption of a nonindigenous way of life; her demand for Turtle's assimilation is as much about restoring what has been taken away from her as it is a struggle for "cultural continuity and political autonomy, such as through the rights to raise Native children in tribal communities" (Schultermandl 225).

This contestation extends into a plea to preserve an entire ecosystem that has historically come under threat through institutional discrimination and oppression. If Kingsolver's major theme in *The Bean Trees* is the definition of family as a social unit that transcends the limitations of the patriarchal nuclear structure, then *Pigs in Heaven* strives to take seriously the difference between Taylor and Annawake's ways of understanding the individual's relationship to his or her community. This radical reconsideration of family that Kingsolver undertakes is designed to shake up the reader's basic sense of familial ties and belonging, destabilizing the heteronormative perspective which has been used as a tool for domination and discrimination. For Annawake, "we don't distinguish between father, uncle, mother, grandmother. We don't think of ourselves as having extended families" (*PH* 284). As she details, the importance of family as a bearer of tradition that is crucially at variance from the mainstream is lost when children from her tribe grow up deracinated from their roots: "Federal law put them in boarding school. Cut off their hair, taught them English, taught them to love Jesus, and made them spend their entire childhood in a dormitory. They got to see their people maybe twice a year. Family has always been our highest value, but that generation of kids never learned how to be in a family. The past got broken off" (*PH* 227).

Seen in this way, *Pigs in Heaven* constitutes Kingsolver's desire to broaden her novelistic canvas through writing from the position of the other and mining the resources afforded by seeing the world from the perspective of the other. The recognition that her earlier novel reflects her personal subjectivity as a white woman is modified not only through her presentation of Native Americans as well-rounded characters whose claims and desires are artistically acknowledged as serious and worthy of consideration but also in the patient outlining of the equal *validity* between Annawake and Taylor's respective reasons for claiming Turtle. If Kingsolver can be accused of a problematic reduction of perspective in *The Bean Trees*, she rectifies this limitation by maintaining a dialogicity of perspectives right until the conclusion of *Pigs in Heaven*. As Wagner-Martin notes, this tension causes a good deal of discomfort on Kingsolver's part: "writing *Pigs in Heaven* gave her 'knots' in her stomach because she saw no possible compromise" between the positivity of Taylor's maternal altruism for Turtle and the historical rights of the Cherokees to claim a member of their community as their own (*Barbara Kingsolver's World* 42). By sustaining this contradiction as the backbone of the novel, Kingsolver forces her reader to reevaluate basic moral concepts of goodness and care, frameworks that she left unexplored in the earlier novel. Indeed, Kingsolver veers into the genre of tragedy, defined by the Romantic philosopher Hegel as an unresolved contestation between two equally justified notions of what is right. A conversation between Annawake and Taylor's romantic attachment Jax highlight this painful irreconcilability:

> "I'm trying to see both sides."
> "You can't," Jax says. "And Taylor can't. It's impossible. Your definitions of 'good' are not in the same dictionary. There is no point of intersection in this dialogue." (*PH* 89)

By maintaining her community's rights to "keep its children" under the Indian Child Welfare Act, Annawake defines a different definition of benefit and belonging to the "civilizing" ethos of Western society as enshrined through its legal system (*PH* 64). Once again, this difference proves crucial as a form of resistance against the intellectual justification for colonialization as reflected in the history of the Americas. Robert Williams Jr. comments on this logic as such: "law, regarded by the West as its most respected and cherished instrument of civilization, was also the West's most vital and effective instrument of empire during its genocidal conquest and colonialization of the non-Western peoples of the New World, the American Indians" (6). As I have been analyzing it thus far, it is this clash between the values of the heteronormative reader and an "othered" point of view that allows difference to be productive of multiple perspectives. This survey becomes crucial for Kingsolver in changing attitudes of ownership, exploitation, and rapacious consumption, values that have defined Western frameworks of thought inimical to ecological and social responsibility. If there is a happy ending to be sought that proceeds through legal means, it is (as we will see in the ending of the novel) in an adjudication that combines the universal with the particular, in that it redresses historical injustice while respecting the unquantifiable integrity of human relationships. That Kingsolver achieves this through plot contrivance is not entirely unquestionable; as we will note below, the resolution ironically resurfaces some of the problems that Kingsolver hopes to overcome.

Kingsolver's Idealization of Native American Culture and the Politics of Representation

Kingsolver's attempt to overcome representational bias in the novel is further indexed by her distinction between authentic and inauthentic presentations of Cherokee culture. This resonates with her fictional strategy in general, for Kingsolver insists that writing bears an indelible link to place. In an essay titled "Knowing Our Place," she emphasizes that "the land *still* provides our genesis, however we might like to forget that our food comes from dank, muddy earth. . . . Whether we are leaving it or dealing with an outsider coming into it, it's *here* that matters . . . storytelling is as old as our need to remember where the water is, where the best food grows," demonstrating an awareness about the grounded nature of literary language as repository of climate and heritage (*SW* 39–40).

Kingsolver alerts her reader about the problematic nature of cultural appropriation via a superficial understanding of the culture of the other reinforcing stereotypes which further entrench negative divisions between people. Kingsolver's character Cash Stillwater, a Cherokee who moves to Jackson Hole to find employment, finds himself helping his younger lover Rose do beadwork to sell at the Cheyenne Trading Post. The ubiquity of tourism, and how it contributed to the economy of Jackson Hole at the cost of the welfare of its local residents, is documented by Matthieu F. Brown as such:

> Buried beneath the image of Jackson Hole as an environmentally benign and socially robust community, hides an economic structure that contradicts the wealth Jackson exudes. The transformation of Jackson into a year round tourist center put an end to the off-season in which the residents of Jackson Hole claimed the town as their own. Consequently, Jackson residents were forced into a position of being surrounded by, and sometimes having to serve, tourists nearly twelve months in a year. The resort infrastructure also required outside capital which rushed into Jackson causing locals and neonatives to lose further control of the town. (591)

This displacement, which is driven by the brutal logic of capitalist demand and the desire to exoticize geographical peripheries, leads to a mindset of commodification that reinforces racial stereotypes. Kingsolver criticizes this attitude by satirizing the need of Rose's boss, Mr. Crittenden, to pander to the tourists who have come to visit an "authentic" representation of Indian traditional craftsmanship. As Rose details, Mr. Crittenden "make[s] her sit at a little antique schoolroom desk in the bay-window storefront, where tourists can behold a genuine Indian hunched over her beadwork, squinting in the bad glare" (*PH* 111). Kingsolver acknowledges that the tendency to exoticize and simplify the complex heritage and history of the American Indian plays a major role in an outsider's desire to understand and access their lived experience; Cash himself notes that "the Indian look is evidently big in Europe, where they don't have any Indians" (*PH* 117). We may read *Pigs in Heaven* as Kingsolver's response to this reductiveness, for what she foregrounds in the novel is fiction's ability to increase an aesthetic and moral response to the specificity of the environment as experienced by the other. This respect for otherness in turn deepens our attention toward and care for the embeddedness of human beings in their respective environments. As if to reinforce this point, Kingsolver adds an ironic comment about the presence of McDonald's "in every country in the world" (*PH* 117): the global symbol of American easy consumerism and cultural imperialism provides an ironic counterpoint to the loss of rootedness within a particular climate.

If Cash is placed by Kingsolver to provide ironic commentary, he also functions as a positive conduit to her presentation of Indian culture through the stomp dance. As he invites Alice to participate in this ceremony, Kingsolver is able to illustrate the thoughts and feelings of a white woman approaching this event in a respectful fashion. Reading Kingsolver's depiction of the stomp dance reveals an emphasis on interconnectedness and togetherness, concepts that have been positive traits in her envisioning of community. Alice feels an affective connection with the spiritual power of the ceremony in a way that transcends language and breaks down the barriers between the solipsistic ego and its surroundings: "Alice feels transported. . . . His words blend together into an unbroken song, as smooth as water over stones. It is a little like those holy-roller churches she loved, where, when someone fell into a swoon, you *felt* their meaning; in the roof of your mouth and your fingertips you felt it, without needing to separate out the particular words" (*PH* 268). This feeling of participation microcosmically provides a utopic image of what society should be. For Kingsolver, the American Indian community functions almost as an antidote to American individualism and unfettered exploitation. Indeed, Kingsolver draws upon an alternative representation of interrelation which stresses symbiotic dependence between the human being and his or her environment; as the Native American poet Paula Gunn Allen writes in her book *The Sacred Hoop*, "at base, every story, every song, every ceremony tells the Indian that each crea-ture is part of a living whole and that all parts of that whole are related to one another by virtue of their participation in the whole of being. . . . The circle of being is not physical, but it is dynamic and alive" (241).

However, Kingsolver's literary strategy here runs into problems, and critics have accused her of romanticizing and idealizing the Cherokee. For these read-ers Kingsolver is guilty of appropriating the culture of the other for her ends in her attempt to "play" Cherokee. Peter Bayers argues that "although well-intentioned, Kingsolver's novel runs into representational problems in regard to her portrayals of Natives, despite her efforts to challenge those representations overtly . . . in the end it still romanticizes and idealizes Natives, reinscribing the cultural hegemony of Euroamerican imaginings of Native American peoples" (37). Kathleen Godfrey provides a more scathing critique of Kingsolver, argu-ing that she employs Eurocentric rhetorical devices throughout *Pigs In Heaven* that paint the American Indian as being closer to nature and more communal, essentializing a timeless ethnic identity that is clearly divorced from reality. In an attempt to attenuate this criticism, Michael posits that Kingsolver "does not so much play on stereotypes as point to the possibilities that accompany a worldview that values the collective and conceives of the individual as inextri-cable from the community" (106). My own viewpoint with respect to this issue is that the difference between two modes of understanding individuality and its relationship to community (autonomous and self-centered vs. fragile and code-pendent) allows Kingsolver the intellectual and artistic space to conceptualize the gap between what society is and what society can be.

In this way the utopic bent in the early fiction does not so much render a simplistic understanding of political perfectibility as it unearths a changed image of society from within. In novels that go out of their way to question and destabilize conventional beliefs about personal ownership and social organiza-tion, it is Kingsolver's insistence on difference as realizable alternative that drive her ethical concerns with issues of gender, race, and class in contemporary America. In short her aim is to unsettle and defamiliarize, not sentimentalize. By turning finally to the conclusion of *Pigs in Heaven* and the way Kingsolver achieves resolution to the problem of Turtle's custody through a novel and sur-prising union, I argue that Kingsolver's aim to recalibrate justice in a way that stresses *both* personal dignity and collective responsibility, an ending that rings true to the thematic threads she weaves throughout Taylor's narrative.

Justice, Identity, and the Image of the Future Generation
The fortuitous patterning of happy circumstance as narrative artifice indicates the importance Kingsolver places on resolution, and how the narrative has been

"engineered" to achieve this. More concretely Annawake plays matchmaker by setting up a romantic union between Alice and Cash. In doing so the tribal court is able to award joint custody of Turtle to Taylor and Cash, after finding out that he is Turtle's biological grandfather. Through the novel's happy ending, Kingsolver arranges Shakespearean motifs of the discovery of familial ties and marital union as images of social harmony to strike a comfortable balance between Annawake's demands regarding Turtle's reinstatement within the Cherokee, and Taylor's maternal claims upon her adopted child. As Annawake remarks, "what we have to do is to satisfy the requirements of the tribe, without separating Turtle completely from the mother and grandmother she's come to love and trust" (*PH* 338).

What thus transpires through the ending is a presentation of "family" commodious enough to place Taylor's personal desires with respect to motherhood within allegiance to the tribe. As Michael comments, "what this court decision asks for is an openness to a much expanded notion of extended family that crosses cultures and makes room for connections based on caring, on genealogy, and on shared cultural heritage" (107). The utter importance placed on union and communion necessitates a rethinking of individual identity: Alice has to abandon her erstwhile self-reliance predicated upon the idea that she "could go on for thirteen generations without no men" (*PH* 27) through her marriage with Cash, and Turtle recognizes that "from now until the end of time she is connected to this family that's parading down Main Street" (*PH* 341). Kingsolver ensures that the decisions mother and daughter make are validated through the positive portrayals of warmth, conviviality, and unselfishness demonstrated by the Cherokee people (Alice pointedly observes how Cherokee adolescent boys are "demonstrating love" in a manner that counteracts acculturated masculine aggression [*PH* 222]). She emphasizes this through the figure of Cash, who combines masculine independence with feminine virtues of modesty, politeness, and domesticity.

To put it simply, Kingsolver offers to her reader an ideal vision of community that combines respect for diversity and difference with synthesis. This image of heterogeneity reminds us that "America is [not] all one country" (*PH* 227). The fact that the court decision foregrounds hybridity over essentialism (Turtle's extended family cuts across racial boundaries and bloodlines) forms part of Kingsolver's aim to destabilize racial constructs tied to a set of cultural norms and expectations. As Taylor herself muses at one point, "maybe being Indian isn't any one thing, any more than being white is one thing" (*PH* 95). The deconstruction of essentialism thereby points to a new notion of belonging, wherein group identity transcends the narrow boundaries of race, class, and genealogy. Once again, the Cherokee people supply the ideal image of this union: Annawake states that her tribe is "not into racial purity" and that "being Cherokee is more or less a mind-set" (*PH* 278, 275). As Circe Sturm remarks, the Cherokee people are "remarkable for having no minimum biogenetic standard, no minimum degree of blood, for citizenship" (89). Indeed, this hospitality is played out in the court decision which crucially seeks to "fashion an appropriate remedy" to the hurt and trauma begun prior to Turtle's abandonment, rather than punitively cast judgment and punishment (*PH* 318).

What the decision effects is, on the one hand, a validation of Taylor's identity as defined and marked by her narrative she shares with Turtle, and on the other hand, a recognition that her struggles and decisions are constantly mediated by the members of her community she becomes linked to as their collective stories draw to a close. In this way Kingsolver positions the court decision as the natural culmination of Taylor's narrative, for it suitably embeds Taylor's receiving of "the absolute power of motherhood" (*PH* 341), which started *The Bean Trees,* within a larger, historical narrative of loss and recovery. This serves to drive home the message about "how your kids aren't really *yours,* they're just these people that you try to keep an eye on . . . everything you ever get is really just on loan" (*BT* 244). Kingsolver's understanding of stewardship and protection mitigates against Kristina Fagan's strident critique of the ending of *Pigs in Heaven.* For Fagan, "Kingsolver avoids the task of imagining how Native people and settlers can learn to live together as large communities . . . a big part of the appeal of this novel comes from the way it sidesteps big issues [of land rights, constitutional changes] by working them out in a way that is apparently natural. The reader is reassured that all the ethical and cultural conflicts that the book lays out can be solved by individual acts of love" (260).

Kingsolver answers this criticism by showing how these "acts of love" are a motivated and complex response toward the urgent needs of the vulnerable. By wrestling with the definitions of "good" and "care" throughout *Pigs in Heaven,* Kingsolver demonstrates how characters come together to work though the baggage and burden of the past by finding common ground rooted in concrete, "doable" actions that ameliorate, rather than provide an unrealistic panacea. Once again difference supplies an important ethical model of relationality in place of a hierarchical imbalance that justifies domination rather than respectful coexistence. *Pigs In Heaven* signals Kingsolver's willingness to imagine otherness as changed image of the possible, of utopia as a literary registering of both the plausibility and necessity of a critique of the present through an unsettling transposition.

As I have argued in this chapter, *The Bean Trees* and *Pigs in Heaven* form two parts of an extended narration about Taylor Greer. Kingsolver's early focus on a single female character anchoring the thematic elements of her diptych enables the reader to follow a drama of development and maturity that culminates in a happy reintegration within an America whose cultural and spiritual geography are similarly regenerated to suggest futural possibilities for the enactment of social justice and political redressal. To put forth a utopic picture of nonviolent belonging, nurturance, and coexistence within an ecosystem that is both fragile and resilient, Kingsolver destabilizes some of the basic impetuses of imperious subjectivity—ownership, possession over objects and resources within the environment, and the need for consumption. By doing so she recalibrates our collective expectations about what healthy human growth and development entails, while suggesting new patterns of adaptation and flourishing in the context of an ecological totality that sustains us as much as we contribute toward its vitality.

The next chapter develops Kingsolver's feminist impetuses by considering how the presentation of female subjectivity contributes toward a complex understanding of narrative form. By extending narratorial perspective from being heavily focalized through one character to take in multiple, dissonant female voices that continually subvert expectations of closure derived from a controlling masculine ideological perspective, Kingsolver continues her exploration of alternative modes of cognition and ways of knowing and controlling reality. It is therefore the feminine voice that forms the site of a struggle between the masculine imposition of knowledge and the achievement of self-understanding at variance with, but never completely divorced from, this gendered containment. Shifting between deficiency and excess, the next chapter will position *Animal Dreams* and *The Poisonwood Bible* as narratives that connect gender, politics, and narrative structure as interlinked and overdetermined by Kingsolver's urge to reimagine lost possibilities and moments of change.

CHAPTER 3

Trauma and the Female Voice
Animal Dreams and *The Poisonwood Bible*

Kingsolver's engagement with the political crises and turmoil of the twentieth century deeply informs her literary view of novel-writing as a means by which to access alternative accounts of history, a perspective that as much informs the trenchant critique of African colonialism in *The Poisonwood Bible* as it does the representation of American postwar paranoia against communism in *The Lacuna*. These imaginative reconstructions turn muteness and disability into potent tropes for truths that have been repressed by hegemonic power structures. To this end her employment of multiple perspectives in *Animal Dreams* and *The Poisonwood Bible* forms part of her strategy to destabilize any monolithic account of historical responsibility that neatly and obdurately separates victor from victim, hero from villain. Placing these two novels in conversation with each other demonstrates Kingsolver's complex use of the female narrative voice. This artistic strategy aptly registers the impact of sufferings inflicted upon the natural and maternal body by historical and political processes of violence. Its fragility is then harnessed to uncover "skeletons in the civic closet" (*AD* 321), which have, in the two novels, been corporeally and symbolically maimed and mutilated by their subjugation under patriarchy.

Kingsolver brings with her an ecofeminist self-consciousness about the extent to which literary tradition has inflected language with the discourses of male-centered privilege that justifies domination and silencing. The scarring of the landscape in Gracela and the Congo is registered both as environmental degradation and psychic wounding. In response to this wounding, the female voice strives to write back to this lineage of exclusion. As Orleanna Price notes, she "was lodged in the heart of darkness, so thoroughly bent to the shape of

marriage" (*PB* 201). While both novels consistently return to themes of physical and mental disability and deformity, they also demonstrate how Kingsolver
returns a vision of truth to the witnessing of historical circumstance which is
provisional and accretive rather than unbending and unrelentingly myopic. An
ecofeminist perspective can thus suggest how the muteness of the natural and
feminine body can answer back to patriarchy via a creative transformation of
language *outside* of conceptual paradigms. Just as the women in Gracela attempt to compose "a written history of Grace and its heroic struggle against
the Black Mountain Mining Company" (*AD* 200) as an act of resistance, the
rubbing-off of viewpoints in *The Poisonwood Bible* creates a dialogic space of
re-inscription wherein alternative personal histories of feminine suffering can
be told at a variance from the official accounts of American involvement in the
postcolonial politics of Africa.

Kingsolver voices this ethos in an essay titled "The Spaces Between,"
wherein she states that "to write novels, to design a museum, to teach fourth-
graders about history—all these enterprises require the interpretation of other
lives. And all of them, historically, have been corrupted by privileges of race,
class, and gender" (*HT* 153). As I will note below, Kingsolver's fictional ethics
are informed both by an existential and utopian thrust. If novel-writing is to
authentically "represent the world I can see and touch as honestly as I know
how," (*HT* 154) then it must struggle with an enlarged notion of responsibility
and accountability that suggests that "everyone is complicit" with the continued failure of utopian politics and betrayal of humanistic ideals through greed,
self-centeredness, and moral blindness (*PB* 538). This pragmatic assessment
of the gap between rhetoric and reality lends a trenchant political dimension
to Kingsolver's constant representation of place in her fiction, one that (in the
context of the two novels under analysis in this chapter) connects personal
memory with the trauma and loss that are silently etched onto the landscape,
which at once offers shelter and resists assimilation.

Kingsolver tempers this existential reading of the relationship between personal action and historical narrative by emphasizing the necessity of a clarified
aesthetic vision gained through accessing the stories one "hasn't heard yet"
(*HT* 156). This can allow one to negotiate multiple versions of truth as a necessary bulwark against ideological narrowness and moral absolutism. What this
ultimately implies is an awareness about our sense of home and its contested
boundaries as part of the universal and globalized: we cannot *not be* cognizant
of the violence we enact upon the land through our activity in shaping personal
and collective history, even though nationalistic and religious rhetoric anaesthe-
tizes us as to our culpability. In so doing, Kingsolver politicizes the everyday by
situating the American domicile and interrogating its ideological foundations

within the foreign: the narrative of *Animal Dreams* is constantly haunted by the absence of Hallie Noline, who sacrifices her safety to assist Nicaraguan farmers in the fight against government forces threatening their livelihoods, and *The Poisonwood Bible* records the increasing disorientation and ultimate disillusionment of its characters in the heart of a Congo in the throes of upheaval and transformation. As Kristen Jacobson notes, "Kingsolver's fiction engages the 'translocal' home and redefines conventional American domesticity's boundaries by explicitly and self-consciously locating home within national and global political contexts" ("Imagined Geographies" 180). These shifting sites of self-definition influence the narrative structures of the two novels under analysis to the extent that they highlight fragmentation as a mode of negotiating with the trauma of the past which can only enter narrative as belated translation and recuperation of the traumatic event.

Kingsolver's handling of traumatic experiences links her female narrators together as characters at once defined by their pasts and free to refashion their identities in creative and life-affirming ways in the aftermath of their experiences. Once again, Kingsolver's fiction evinces an ethical dimensionality that suggests not repressing trauma but instead negotiating guilt and responsibility as ways we can grow out of the hurt of the past. Indeed, trauma and the female subject are themes closely associated in *Animal Dreams* and *The Poisonwood Bible*, as Kingsolver presents her reader with examples of coping with trauma that ironically chart out a clarified moral vision that is birthed from authentic witnessing. As Langdon Elsbree points out, it is because the female subject "cherishes intimacy [and] accepts vulnerability" that it is more capable of processing the almost unbearable subjective aftereffects of trauma that becomes im*print*ed on both body and language (34). This sentiment is aptly registered by Adah Price, one of the five female narrators of *The Poisonwood Bible*, who notes that "we are the balance of our damage and our transgressions," the uneasy oscillation between deficiency and excess encoding the delayed impact of trauma that can never be experienced directly (*PB* 533). As we will see below, Kingsolver's literary achievement is to use narrative perspective to foreground the performative aspects of living with trauma as it is inflected through "the effort of remembrance and witnessing, unresolved fear, anger and grief" (Stevenson 88). What the reader encounters through Kingsolver's female narrators whose voices are intermittently punctured with gaps, indeterminacies, and evasions are life stories of hurt and coping with pain, attempts at coming to terms with the past that emphasize the marking of history on psychic experiences.

At the same time, Kingsolver's adoption of multiple narrative focalizers whose individual identities have been shaped by this history in different ways is crucial in destabilizing the realist tradition of the omniscient narrator who controls the interpretation of the diegesis. In contrast to clear-cut political divisions that fueled the geopolitical tensions of the Cold War and justify systems of extractive exploitation, Kingsolver's politics of the novel is tied to her use of multiple narrators who "reveal to one another . . . their own foundational truths, the subversive currents of personal truths that run underneath the official version" (Austenfeld 298). Indeed, just as Kingsolver's narratives struggle to break free from the classic realist novel, her characters attempt to move beyond definitional categories to enunciate an existential truth that remains authentic to their exceptional circumstances and experiences. As Breyan Strickler argues, "healing occurs for [Kingsolver's] women when they free themselves from the confines of [hegemonic] discourse through a process of deconstruction akin to rebirth" (112). This "deconstruction" of identity cannot be separated from facing up to the pain of the past, and in so doing, constructing new modes of being that allow the past to be encountered in a new context.

As Kingsolver sees it, this personal emancipation politicizes our collective relationship to the past, as it allows us to understand America's culpability in a historical context (as misguided arbiter in African politics as part of a response to the Cold War) and in a contemporary setting (involvement in Nicaragua). Just as the characters in the novels move from incomprehension and denial to understanding and commitment, Kingsolver enunciates the fact that in revisiting the past, "awareness is everything," both on a personal as well as on a political level (*AD* 324). In opposition to forgetting (which for Kingsolver is always associated with a diminishment of self and moral responsibility), the novels seek to ask questions about how society can fruitfully "acknowledge [its] larger agenda than to pretend it doesn't exist" (*SW* 107–8).

Codi Noline's Sense of Self and Place in *Animal Dreams*

Kingsolver's novel charts a narrative of displacement and return through the experiences of Codi Noline, whose sense of betrayal and abandonment form powerful reasons for her initial departure from Grace, Arizona. Her narrative is counterpointed by a more impressionistic rendering of the slowly degenerating mind of Codi's father Homer Noline, who is suffering from an onset of Alzheimer's disease. Kingsolver's interest in the urgency and fragility of memory is evident in the characters' obsessive fixations with the past and their failure to move past certain traumatic memories that bind together collective histories of pain and neglect. Wagner-Martin aptly points out that Kingsolver is writing about "the way that loss of memory is the loss of self, both for a culture and an individual" (*Barbara Kingsolver's World* 56): what trauma theory provides to her presentation of Codi is the paradoxical tension between the "resistance to facing painful, disturbing knowledge" (Stevenson 88) in the effort to reconnect with the place of her childhood, and the necessity of remembering and witnessing to these incidents as indelible parts of her personal narrative—dealing with the past is what opens up a future. Kingsolver's narrative technique becomes important in allowing her reader to participate in the working-out of trauma from Codi's perspective: the defining moments of her past are linguistically transmitted through repetitions, elisions, and flashbacks that remain frustratingly incomplete until Codi is ready to assume a fuller definition of subjectivity as an expectant mother and partner to Loyd Peregrina.

Codi's mixing of memory and fantasy comes out most clearly in one of her main fixations of the past: the untimely death of her mother from kidney failure, and the dramatic attempt to evacuate her via helicopter for medical aid. As it precipitates in Codi's recollection, the representation of the evacuation sits uneasily between a factual account and her own reconstruction of it, between personal trauma and the community's witnessing of the event:

> One of my few plain childhood memories was of that day. I was not quite three, Hallie was newborn, and I'm told I couldn't possibly remember it because I wasn't there. The picture I have in my mind is nevertheless clear: two men in white pants handling the stretcher like a fragile, important package. The helicopter blade beating, sending out currents of air across the alfalfa field behind the hospital. This was up above the canyon, in the days when they grew crops up there. The flattened-down alfalfa plants showed their silvery undersides in patterns that looked like waves. The field became the ocean I'd seen in storybooks, here in the middle of the desert, like some miracle.
>
> Then the rotor slowed and stopped, setting the people in the crowd to murmuring: What? Why? And then the door opened and the long white bundle of my mother came out again, carried differently now, no longer an urgent matter.
>
> According to generally-agreed upon history, Hallie and I were home with a babysitter. This is my problem—I clearly remember things I haven't seen, sometimes things that never happened. (*AD* 48–49)

As the passage implies, Codi's fallible memory of the incident, and her disavowal as to its veracity, is arguably a psychological coping mechanism for the screening-out of its traumatic impact. At the same time, motifs of rescue (with the helicopter arriving to save Codi's mother) and the vulnerability of the infirm form an undercurrent connecting this memory to Codi's other memory of her and Hallie endeavoring to save a litter of coyote puppies from a flood: as Codi mentions, "as plainly as anything then, I remembered trying to save the coyotes from the flood" (*AD* 196). This permeability of memory not only signals Kingsolver's interest in exploring psychological tension and the impact of time upon personality, but also suggests how individual narratives are collectively defined by a shared psychic inheritance and burden.

Indeed, the death of Codi and Hallie's mother resonates in the memories of Codi and Homer, linking their narratives together as shared attempts to come to terms with the void her death leaves in their lives. The sections of the novel that are focalized through Homer blend reminiscence with a disordered melding between present impression and past obsession, as Homer is haunted both by his wife's passing and the stillbirth of Codi's child, another incident she manages to repress. For Homer, these two incidents are fatally linked, resulting in a depressive state of mind chained to the idea of time and generativity as dead repetition of traumatic wounding: "The ghost of their happiest time returned to inhabit the miserable body of their child. He can't help feeling he has damaged them all, just by linking them together. His family is a web of women dead and alive, with himself at the center like a spider" (*AD* 100). Through Homer's narratorial perspective, Kingsolver reveals a nexus of pain and unresolved guilt that has irrevocably strained the relationship between father and daughter (Codi opines at one point that "my relationship with Doc Homer has always improved with distance" [*AD* 10]), while also uncovering more hidden sources of Codi's vexed relationship to the community of Grace. Codi's self-isolation can be read as one more compromise-formation she psychologically constructs to deal with the traumatic impact of loss, as both father and daughter are trapped by the notion that to love means to open oneself out to the devastating possibility of absence: "God, why does a mortal man have children? It is senseless to love anything this much" (*AD* 21).

However, while Homer is never afforded the opportunity to move beyond this sterile repetition that defines his psyche, Codi senses that there is something more to be gained through a renewed attachment to the place of her past. As Stevenson argues, "[Homer's] confused thoughts reveal aspects of Codi's past that she has repressed, yet he loses the ability to bring order to his memories and impressions, and thus loses himself. . . . In contrast, Codi moves toward memory regained, a process that involves reconstructing her past, her place within Grace, and her identity" (89). As always with Kingsolver, this reattachment can only come about through being able to appreciate otherness as integral to the reevaluation of the fundamental tenets of personhood and subjectivity. To be sure, Codi intuits the necessity of belonging to a place, and in so doing, claiming the past as authentically one's own: in a letter written to Hallie, she notes that "*my life is a pitiful, mechanical thing without a past*" (*AD* 205), and in a conversation with Loyd about his Pueblo heritage, she says that "I guess I'm nothing. The Nothing Tribe" (*AD* 220). In fact, Codi's family name is already marked with separateness and disavowal: ashamed by a marriage between one of the Gracela sisters (founders of Grace) and his kin, Homer lies about where his family has come from, insisting instead that they belong to Illinois.

It is then in the attempt of the narrative to overcome this feeling of displacement and deracination that its affective reach lies. As Kingsolver gradually implies, it will be up to Loyd to heal the rift between Codi and the "memory minefield" (*AD* 47) that Grace represents for her. In doing so he enlarges her sense of place, urging her to see the land as a site of both destruction and renewal. As with Kingsolver's other positive representations of Native American men, Loyd effortlessly and naturally combines the virtues of masculinity and femininity, embodying a virility associated with labor while being honest and vulnerable enough to change his attitudes toward cockfighting after listening to Codi's reservations about animal cruelty. Naomi Jacobs further elaborates upon the symbolic significance of Loyd in terms of Kingsolver's interest in a utopic alliance between civilization and the natural environment: "Loyd is associated with both wild nature and domesticity. His family name, Peregrina, evokes the wild falcon that always returns to its original nesting grounds. His constant companion is a coyote/dog cross, again a mix of the wild and domesticated" (3). Once again we note how Kingsolver's utopianism is embedded within the realistic, with her pragmatic acknowledgement of deep-seated sources of violence and injustice not taking away from her belief that fiction provides "a house of open passage" (*HT* 156) out of entrenched systems of oppression. As Robin Cohen writes, Loyd squarely stands for "a new age and a better world" (151). Most important, Loyd represents a way out of traumatic fixation for Codi, because he is *both* the father of the stillborn infant Codi has lost, and the parent of her new baby: in the redemptive logic of the novel, loss is ultimately replaced by gain, a movement toward a rehabilitation of the body and the spirit.

In this way Loyd plays Virgil to Codi's Dante, leading her on an exploration of Pueblo custom and culture that allows her to envision alternative ways of being. Two important moments occur that reorientate Codi's understanding of the relationship between life and death, nature and human habitation, realms that have traditionally been viewed as dichotomous in the Western imagination. The first occurs during the festival of the Day of the Dead, which commemorates familial love and memory in ways that break down the boundaries between life and death. In contrast to Homer's overt repudiation of his past (and his barring his children from visiting the gravesite of their ancestors), participation in the festival enables Codi to rethink loss as complete absence and ineluctable mourning. As she observes, "it was a comfort to see this attention lavished on the dead. In these families you would never stop being loved" (*AD* 168). It is therefore no coincidence that Codi learns about the histories of the Nolinas and the Gracela sisters at the cemetery where the festival is held—as Vicky Newman writes, "it is in the cemeteries that [Codi] begins to unfold the silenced histories of her life and of the community to which she has returned" (110). She grows to understand that death and the past can be integrated into life in ways that emphasize transformation rather than tragic division.

Kingsolver focuses the permeability between life and death as representative of an acceptance of loss, and the rehabilitation of memory as loving commemoration, in an image that suggests rebirth within Codi: "Golden children ran wild over a field of dead great-grandmothers and great-grandfathers, and the bones must have wanted to rise up and knock together and rattle with joy. I have never seen a town that gave so much—so much of what *counts*—to its children" (*AD* 170). This expanded sense of place as "an organic entity that supports communal identity" (Rubenstein 39) allows her to be receptive to Loyd's explanation of the significance of Pueblo architecture in the second moment I will focus on. This happens as Codi accompanies him into the desert and notices "a village built into the cliff . . . [with] multistory apartments and unbelievably careful masonry" (*AD* 218). As Loyd points out, the habitation being built does not attempt to dominate and use up natural resources for its own ends; instead it is held in an "embrace" by "the perfect constructions of nature," (*AD* 218) with the sentiment echoing Homer's earlier claim that "probably there is no real invention . . . just a good deal of elaboration on nature" (*AD* 75). Put more metaphorically it will be in Codi's acceptance of how Grace has indelibly defined her family that she can start to build solid existential foundations in the locale.

These two moments aptly combine to chart Codi's growing awareness that our sense of home and belonging cannot be separated from an existence fully and entirely rooted within the fragility of place. As Wagner-Martin notes, "the disillusionment and angst that mark Codi's response to much of life have no place in an active, and involved, participatory life" (*Barbara Kingsolver's World* 57). As I have argued earlier on in this chapter, Kingsolver subscribes to an existentialist ethos of action, which states that it is only in commitment and choice that ethics and politics are authentically possible. What Codi ultimately learns is that to "feel like [a place] *wants* to take me in" (*AD* 187) is secondary to a capacity to construct a way of belonging: whatever "order in the cosmos" (*AD* 13) we can discern is defined solely through the sum-total of human intervention and responsible decision-making. Kingsolver thereby has in Codi voice the novel's ethical vision as such: "morality is not a large, constructed *thing* you have or have not, but simply a capacity. Something you carry with you in your brain and hands" (*AD* 243). This applies consistently across her fiction, where Kingsolver insists that intervention occurs through the small, practical altruistic gestures characters make. In the context of *Animal Dreams*, the character who best embodies this fierce commitment to action is Hallie Noline, and it is in her tragedy that cathartic resolution for Codi becomes possible.

Hallie's practical commitment to aiding farmers in Nicaragua with her agricultural expertise provides the novel with an example of individualistic intervention that balances idealism with a realistic understanding of the conditions that impede change and necessitate action. As Codi comments, "the tragedy for Hallie was that there might never be a cause worth risking everything for in our lifetime" (*AD* 36). Although Hallie never physically appears as a character within the narrative, Kingsolver makes her an equal, if not more powerful, foil to Codi's lassitude and cynicism through letters that locate an ecological and political crisis outside of Grace that she ultimately feels responsible for. In an essay titled "Careful What You Let In The Door," Kingsolver details her personal investment in the real-world politics of harm she brings into the novel as such:

> It mattered to me, for example, that we citizens of the U.S. bought guns and dressed up an army that killed plain, earnest people in Nicaragua who were trying only to find peace and a kinder way of life. I wanted to bring that evil piece of history into a story, in a way that would make a reader feel sadness and dread but still keep reading, becoming convinced it was necessary to care. So I invented Hallie Noline, and caused her to die. I did it because this happened, not to imaginary Hallie but to thousands of real people. (*HT* 255)

In fact, as Wagner-Martin details, "the novel's dedication [is] to Ben Linder, an Oregon engineering student who, while helping to build a hydroelectric dam in Nicaragua, had been shot in the head by Contras" (*Barbara Kingsolver's World* 60). As we have seen, Kingsolver decries the separation of aesthetics from politics by using novel-writing as a powerful forum for raising awareness about the culpability of the American government, which has not assumed responsibility for regimes of oppression and violence it has participated in for ideological reasons.

In the context of the novel, this baleful repression is presented in terms of a forgetting. Hallie comments that "we were a nation in love with forgetting the facts" (*AD* 62) and that America is *"a nation of amnesiacs,"* (*AD* 205) emphasizing Kingsolver's ethical point that it is only by remembering the past and claiming responsibility for that history that change is possible: what Codi manages to achieve on a personal level, America's political leadership has failed to do with respect to its national consciousness. If *Animal Dreams* and *The Poisonwood Bible* can be read as "political novels," they function to (re)examine the political and religious ideals that serve to justify sacrificing human and nonhuman lives for nationalistic or ideological gain. Hallie's uncovering of the damage that is done to the Nicaraguan ecosystem, and the political machinery that supports this pillage, serves to speak an inconvenient truth to power. She can be likened to the Athenian philosopher Socrates, who was put to death by the state because of his constant upsetting of misplaced complacency and moral obtuseness by asking difficult questions about the status quo, thereby exposing the inauthentic rhetoric that lies behind the facade of power and privilege. Codi says just as much in her reminiscence about her younger sister: "But a nation gloats on the hostility of its enemies, while Hallie had proven the malevolence of some men we supplied with machine guns. Hallie was a skeleton in the civic closet" (*AD* 321).

Indeed, Hallie's mission resonates with Kingsolver's artistic ethos insofar as both understand the necessity of awakening others from their dogmatic slumber and allowing them to approach ethical relationality and ecological belonging from new perspectives. Hallie opines that "*it's easy to get used to the privilege of a safe life*" (*AD* 90), eschewing the unjustified comforts of domesticity to involve herself with the struggle for a better future for peoples whose traditional ways of life are being eroded and destroyed. Kingsolver herself states in an essay titled "Jabberwocky" that "art is the antidote that can call us back from the edge of numbness, restoring the ability to feel for another. By virtue of that power, it is political" (*HT* 232). Art thereby allows its reader to see differently as the necessary accompaniment to encountering otherness as a conduit to changing preestablished notions of right and wrong. As we will see in our analysis of *The Poisonwood Bible*, it is the characters who stubbornly fail to adjust and enlarge their moral compasses and sensibilities who are destroyed. As Kingsolver sees it, the capacity for change defines the essence of a responsible politics, and happily mitigates against fatalistic and deterministic accounts of history: we need the perspective provided by art that allows otherness to "speak back" to us to access history differently.

Kingsolver condenses the urgent need for art to broaden ethical understanding toward the end of "Jabberwocky" in ways that resonate with Hallie's motivations, and with (as we will see later) what the Price daughters take away with them from their extreme experiences in Kilanga: "Good art is political, whether it means to be or not, insofar as it provides the chance to understand points of view alien to our own. Its nature is the opposite of spiritual meanness, bigotry, and warfare. If it is disturbing at times, or unpalatable, it may be a good idea to buy it anyway" (*HT* 234). What Hallie ultimately espouses is a practical, manageable ethics of action that cannot be divorced from ameliorating concrete conditions. This intervention is based not on grandiose political belief, but instead on the virtues of careful observation and attentiveness to the ways wherein the symbiotic relationship between human beings and their ecosystems manifests itself within an ecosystem. Indeed, Hallie enunciates this truth in a letter to Codi, in which she replaces the absolutism of value systems with the accretive force of daily nurturance, actions that helpfully foster the utopic vision Kingsolver hinges her novelistic craft on: "*You're thinking of revolution as a great all-or-nothing. I think of it as one more morning in a muggy cotton field, checking the undersides of leaves to see what's been there, figuring out what to do that won't clear a path for worse problems next week. . . . The daily work—that goes on* [italics in the original]" (*AD* 305).

Place, and our attitude toward it, become the fundamental ethical grounds through which political practice can be altered for the better. Kingsolver demonstrates how observation and awareness function as motors for informed resistance through Codi's pedagogic role as a science teacher. At first, she bemoans the fact that she has to "get people interested in animals which have no discernable heads, tails, fins, or the like" (*AD* 111); however, as she grows into her role as educator, she succeeds in opening her students' eyes to invisible ecosystems that have come under threat by a mining company that is poisoning the water supply in order to extract more copper. As her science experiments confirm this fact, she is invited to speak to more people in the community so as to highlight the urgent need for action. In line with the novel's positive focus on action as defining an individual's sense of purpose, Codi's conscientiousness allows her to define her role within the community she is at first ambivalent toward. By the end of the novel, she proudly affirms that her vocation is to teach her future students to be "custodians of the earth" (*AD* 342). For Kingsolver, this ethic of stewardship aligns gentleness with "cultural memory," (*AD* 342) for the commemoration of tradition reminds the individual that he or she is nothing more than a "permanent houseguest" (*AD* 247) within an ecosystem that must be preserved and handed down properly to the next generation.

The novel's other vehicle for change stems from a group of women who collectively call themselves the "Stitch-and-Bitch" club. Galvanized by Codi's presentation of the threat posed by Black Mountain Mining, the women lay plans to design and sell peacock piñatas, each one "accompanied by a written history of Grace and its heroic struggles against the Black Mountain Mining

Company" (*AD* 200). Once again, the personal is intertwined with the political, as the integration of the past with the present in the form of a narrative becomes paramount in the attempted preservation of an integral way of life that both precedes and outlasts any single member of the community who participates in it. Kingsolver's presentation of resistance is once again gendered to the extent that it locates effective opposition in the art of craft and care—the piñatas stand for a localized, domestic totality at once fragile and resilient. This point is further emphasized in a conversation the women have with a TV station who have arrived in Grace to bring publicity to their cause. When questioned whether "a piñata can stop a multinational corporation" (*AD* 272), a member of the club replies that "we don't know how to use dynamite. What we know how to do is to make nice things out of paper" (*AD* 273). What this exchange presents is an authentic attestation to the efficacy of action that cannot be separated from the characters' lifeworld—Kingsolver engages with "home not simply as a particular place but as a symbolic space defined through women's traditional domestic tasks and emotional investments" (Rubenstein 39).

Just as Codi's struggles to reconcile images of her traumatic past with the potentialities of a future in Grace is mapped onto the performative unfolding of memory in the consciousnesses of herself and Homer, Kingsolver collates the efforts of Hallie and the women of the Stitch-and-Bitch club so as to tie together action, identity, and belonging. Ultimately Codi finds positive examples of existential commitment in these characters who understand that we all are nothing *outside* of our rootedness to a cause and a reason to defend whatever needs to be defended. This then provides her with the means to work through her trauma in order to witness the gains that have been birthed from absence and pain: as Stevenson opines, "Codi, like many trauma survivors, finds that drawing upon what she has witnessed and learned in order to educate others gives her a sense of hope and purpose" (106).

The novel's final chapter is appropriately titled "Day of All Souls," reflecting a cyclicity by repeating the first chapter of the novel. Moving ahead in time, the reader learns that Homer has died and been buried with the other Nolinas, and that Codi is expecting a child with Loyd. We learn that Codi has been able to finally grieve for the passing of her mother, stillborn child, and Hallie (who has earlier been kidnapped and murdered by hostile forces opposing her work in Nicaragua) by placing their deaths within a fuller context of meaning. This cyclicity not only sustains a thinking of temporality at one with the larger rhythms of the natural world (death, decay, renewal, and rebirth), but also ensures that the future is constantly generated from out of the past. Codi is able to revisit the original sources of her trauma by stepping into her new role as a mother (thereby replacing passive spectatorship of her past with generative agency). This newfound sense of responsibility decenters her erstwhile solipsism, allowing her to finally belong to an existential purpose larger than herself: "You find you're not the center of the universe, suddenly it's all flipped over, you have it in you to be a parent" (*AD* 351). As the last paragraphs of the novel restate, it is in action that redemption from the weight of past tragedy can be sought. Codi now understands that her mother's "act of love" (*AD* 352) in giving birth to her and Hallie, despite the personal sacrifice it entailed, is an act of goodness insofar as Hallie's altruism manifested itself "in the soil of another country" (*AD* 352). Codi can thus peacefully reintegrate the one memory of her mother's death in a life-affirming way: "We're at the edge of the field, far from other people. We stand looking out into the middle of that ocean with alfalfa. I can see my mother there, a small white bundle with nothing left, and I can see that it isn't a tragedy we're watching, really. Just a finished life" (*AD* 352).

In the place of wounding, Codi sees aesthetic completion. *Animal Dreams* posits the therapeutic consequences of immersive and committed action, holding out faith that "it's what you do that makes your soul, not the other way round" (*AD* 344)—individual lives are shaped not only by personal effort, but also by the choices of the people around you. This chapter's focus on the very reality of traumatic memory, and how hurt registers its psychological effects on the subject as a function of body and place, presents a more complex understanding of Kingsolver's politics than that articulated by critics like Krista Comer. For Comer, Kingsolver still resorts to a regressive idealization of landscape, wherein "primitivist representations of society and humans' relationship to land" (92) denote a failed ethical addressal of complex ecocritical problems recognizable to her readers. Apart from speaking to this form of criticism in my outlining of the larger implications of Kingsolver's utopian imaginary, I argue that the presentation of the land in *Animal Dreams* is complexly interwoven with changing definitions of selfhood that are anything but stable, eternal, and essentialist. Comer underestimates Kingsolver's painful negotiation with both historical and geopolitical meaning, ideas that the two novels bring out via the corporeal marking of suffering on body as well as on place. *The Poisonwood Bible* revisits the thematic of action and intervention, but with a more skeptical consciousness as to its morality. In the doomed actions of Nathan Price and his wrongheaded insistence that Congolese society can be shaped and molded through the sheer force of his will, he sacrifices the lives and trust of his family, imbuing them with the "mark" (*PB* 385) of trauma none of them fully escape from. The female voice once again carries the burden of witnessing, destabilizing any single notion of "truth" that can be extracted from it, while offering the possibility that "new artistic conventions [which] encompass both literary and political aims" (Demory 191) can arise from terror, incomprehension, and tragic knowledge.

Language, Resistance, and Traumatic Loss in *The Poisonwood Bible*

The fractured narrative of Kingsolver's *The Poisonwood Bible* succeeds in splintering any single coherent experience of failed Western religious idealism when faced with the alien demands of existentiality in an utterly foreign locale, while managing to weave together a familial history of victims and survivors, perpetrators and sufferers. The novel's employment of five female voices—Orleanna Price, Leah Price, Rachel Price, Adah Price, and Ruth May—recoups a buried legacy of resistance, collaboration, and compromise in order to fold the defeat of the intentions of the familial patriarch into a larger political history of betrayal and unresolved trauma. By telling their narratives in retrospect, Kingsolver allows her characters' final impressions of their time in Kilanga to be refracted by the passing of time and the working-through of pain. Their shifting judgments of their zealous patriarch Nathan Price also enable them to express a growing critical distance from their foundationalist beliefs, which at first anchor them to a narrow, prejudiced view of the world outside of Georgia.

At the same time, Kingsolver's creative handling of the relationship between subjective experience and language positions these five narratives as acts of recovery, performances that suggest how narratorial perspective is both inadequate to and necessary for an ethical engagement with the horrors of the past. As Leah Milne points out, "Kingsolver . . . understand[s] the impossibility of language in wholly depicting the history and collective experience of any country and community, but . . . [ensures] that such histories and experiences no longer remain 'disremembered and unaccounted for'" (367). A multilayered narrative such as in *The Poisonwood Bible* not only emphasizes that there can never be one single "truth" to the experiences the Price family has undergone in the African Congo, but also implies that what matters is "your story, your own slant" (*PB* 495), which is at crucial variance from any official account of history. Indeed, Kingsolver insists that their stories will bear witness to the traumatic transactions enacted upon African soil after "the names of all those conquerors . . . have been erased from our map" (*PB* 445).

Kingsolver's interest in the politics of the Congo nation as part of the historical legacy of Western colonialism naturally leads critical commentary of the novel to classify it as "postcolonial fiction." Kingsolver's cautious use of the term "postcolonial" positions her novel as a uniquely American response to the violence of colonial exploitation that functions as looking glass through which we may understand the country's (in)direct role in this history: "I live in a society that grew prosperous from exploiting others. England has a strong tradition of postcolonial literature but here in the U.S., we can hardly even say the word 'postcolonial.' We like to think we're the good guys. So we persist in our denial, and live with a legacy of exploitation and racial arrogance that continues to tear people apart" (Wagner-Martin, *Barbara Kingsolver's World* 102).

As with her critique of American involvement in Nicaraguan politics in *Animal Dreams*, Kingsolver's aim is to raise awareness about the marking of the colonial experience on the bodies of both aggressor and victim: as Orleanna opines "to live is to be marked," which is the same thing as to "acquire the words of a story" (*PB* 385). Her ethics are thus clearly at diametrical opposition from Rachel's method of coping with trauma: "What happened to us in the Congo was simply the bad luck of two opposite worlds crashing into each other. . . . I ask myself, did I have anything to do with it? The answer is no. . . . Keep my hair presentable and pretend I was elsewhere" (*PB* 465). It is only by recognizing a shared responsibility for faults and transgressions that memories of trauma become an integral part to self-definition. Kingsolver offers this ethical notion of vulnerability as an antidote to what she sees as the worst excesses of American imperialism: as Susan Strehle notes, "American imperialism works to distinguish itself from its European antecedents by championing freedom and democracy . . . claiming benevolence, and asserting that American righteousness makes American acts right" (416). In this way the voice that authentically registers traumatic suffering becomes a politicized site of resistance against structures of power that silence language and bodily experience.

Apart from a common fragility between colonizer and colonized, Kingsolver's "postcolonialism" works to further bolster her interest in hybridity that breaks down ideological barriers between these parties. Sophie Croisy observes that "[Kingsolver's] text is a transcultural one, a kaleidoscopic critique of local cultural heritage and a call for a more schizophrenic envisioning of cultural identity through cultural boundary crossings and beyond cultural absolutism" (224). This hybridity is not only envisioned in the novel by Leah's marriage to Anatole Ngemba (an African schoolteacher and translator for Nathan Price), but also in the polyphonic mixing of languages and cultures that ultimately resists any colonial notion of dominance. Rather than the top-down transmission of truth that obviates genuine exchange between the self and the other, the enlightened missionary Brother Fowles offers an image of the American self that is "the branch that's grafted here, sharing in the richness of these African roots" (*PB* 252).

Fowles's emphasis on decentering the primacy of the subject in an attitude of careful attentiveness toward local conditions mitigate against Nathan's laughable insistence that he can subjugate the Congolese people to his will, imposing American methods upon African mores by growing Georgian crops on foreign soil, determined to "plant his American garden in the Congo" (*PB* 284). Ultimately Kingsolver advocates for what Nathan Kilpatrick calls "a new kind of hybridized life" (104), which (as we have seen so far in this book) embraces difference within the self. In contrast to Nathan, who dies in a half-crazed attempt to carry out baptism in complete ignorance of local trepidation against immersion in water, this multiplicity defines an ethical mode of relationality with the other that opens up a future in the aftermath of trauma. Leah's offspring thus cannot be identified within racial categories; instead, they are "the colors of slit, loam, dust, and clay, an infinite palette for children of their own," (*PB* 526) with Kingsolver's suggestive metaphors implying the *naturality* of diversity and the grounded nature of identity in earthiness.

The Poisonwood Bible also stakes its claim as a "rescripting" of other literary narratives. The intertextual resonances are significant in terms of Kingsolver's questioning of some of the tenets of "high" literary texts whose values might end up alienating the readership she wants to reach. The most noticeable literary precursor that stands behind Kingsolver's novel is Joseph Conrad's novella *Heart of Darkness*, which enlists a similar "framed" narrative in order to chart the dissolution of Western colonial ideals in the Belgian Congo. To be sure, Kingsolver specifically lists Conrad's narrative as one of the texts she consulted while researching and writing her novel (*PB* 545). Her overt allusions to Conrad within her text further consolidates this link: Orleanna observes that she "was lodged in the heart of darkness" (*PB* 201), and Rachel sums up her experiences by characterizing Africa as "darkest" (*PB* 517). Pamela Demory's article "Into the Heart of Light: Barbara Kingsolver Rereads *Heart of Darkness*" is to date the most extended scholarly treatment of the comparisons between Kingsolver and Conrad—for the critic, "Conrad's novella is present as a kind of pre-text of the novel" (181). In Demory's reading, "the multiple narrative perspectives [in *Heart of Darkness* and *The Poisonwood Bible*] suggest the subjectivity of narrative, the impossibility of a story unmediated by someone's personal experiences, and the possibility of multiple truths" (187–88).

Demory is right to highlight that the effects of disorientation that result in both novels due to their complex layering of perspectives which challenge the straightforward understanding of reality and moral absolutes; what Kingsolver draws from Conrad is the notion that literary language can record the interaction between the imagination and experience in ways that allow the reader to confront extreme states of mind. Both texts punch holes in colonial rhetoric by showcasing the moral emptiness of imperialist ideology: as a minor character in Kingsolver's novel observes, "in seventy-five years the only roads the Belgians ever built [in the Congo] are the ones they use to haul out diamonds and rubber" (*PB* 122). Where *The Poisonwood Bible* intervenes as a rescripting of one of the seminal texts of High Modernism is in its allowing full breadth to the female experience of colonial horror. In place of a narrative framed by male storytellers who judge that the harsh "truths" of colonial exploitation are best kept from women residing in the metropole, Kingsolver affords her female characters no such distance from the traumatic impact of the breakdown of their ideals in a land that remains intransigent to shaping.

Indeed, there is no "safe" space for the female characters of Kingsolver's novel wherein their inauthentic ideas about Western civilization can be affirmed: Kingsolver's analogy between patriarchal and colonial domination emphasizes how violence is enacted upon bodies that are passive and silent. As Héloïse Meire points out, "Kingsolver insists on drawing a parallel between the power relationships within the Price family and the power relationships of the colonial and neocolonial powers in the Congo" (75). This parallel highlights not only the absence of female points of view in Conrad, but also a different rendering of the "postcolonial" narrative from a woman's perspective. For Kingsolver, the truths of experience remain deeply tied to a gendered perspective: trauma is registered, encoded, and borne differently for the female subject.

Kingsolver's interest in the relationship between the personal and political reveals itself again in the critical consciousness she brings to bear upon the "domestic." For Jacobson Kingsolver rewrites "conventional domestic fiction like *Little Women* [and its celebration of] the white, middle-class heterosexual family" ("The Neodomestic American Novel" 106). In exposing the shadowy links between bourgeois domesticity and racial privilege, Jacobson convincingly argues that *The Poisonwood Bible* "unmoors domestic fiction's celebration of stable domesticity, exposing its imperial drive and intimate connections with the foreign" ("The Neodomestic American Novel" 108). Apart from exposing America's shameful involvement in the replacing of Patrick Lumumba with the tyrant Mobutu, Kingsolver reveals hidden facets of exploitation and neglect that lie at the very core of our separation of the domestic from the foreign, the personal from the political. In doing so the novel follows the characters' dawning realization that they have all "constructed their lives around a misunderstanding" (*PB* 532).

Kingsolver's critique of Western values strikes at the heart of the most intimate, revealing how "illusions mistaken for truth are the pavement under our feet" (*PB* 532). As we will see, the novel dramatizes a movement from innocence to experience by illustrating how traumatic knowledge destabilizes the very foundations through which the self bases its illusions on. If there is no shelter from these uncomfortable truths that shake up concepts of language and subjectivity, the intimation of these truths holds the promise for an ethical reorientation, one that allows forgiveness for past sins. What each female character learns is therefore nothing less than her capacity for good and evil, being at once chained to "all of [Nathan's] history" (*PB* 533) and free to narrate this history differently.

The Birth of Tragic Awareness in the Price Family
and the Price of Experience and Knowledge

Kingsolver's narrative strategy adds to the literary critique of colonial rapacity by showing how the guilt of the colonizer interacts with personal histories of neglect and betrayal. By registering the physical and psychological trauma of the colonial experience on the Price matriarch Orleanna, Kingsolver allows her elegiac reflections about Nathan and her children to guide her reader's responses toward the events that happened in Kilanga. Orleanna's growth from subservient helpmate into civil-rights activist aptly charts a birth into tragic self-consciousness that interrogates the various forms of dominance and enslavement that must be resisted. As her language suggests, her experiences of loss have afforded her the vantage point through which she understands the link between marital and political violence:

> Maybe I'll even confess the truth, that I rode in with the horsemen and beheld the apocalypse, but still I'll insist I was only a captive witness. What is the conqueror's wife, if not a conquest herself? For that matter, what is *he*? When he rides in to vanquish the untouched tribes, don't you think that they fall down with desire before those sky-coloured eyes? And itch for a turn with those horses, and those guns? That's what we yell back at history, always, always. It wasn't just me; there were crimes strewn six ways to Sunday, and I had my own mouths to feed. I didn't know. I had no life of my own. (*PB* 9)

This dense, lyrical passage ironizes the Christian imagery of the apocalypse in order to suggest a skepticism behind the benevolence of the civilizing mission that forms the ideological backdrop of imperial conquest, as indexed through the heavy-handed vanquishing of the heathen population using mechanized instruments of death. As I have argued above, Kingsolver resolutely refuses the intellectual defense of ignorance and nonculpability: if the same structures of inequality and oppression are reproduced, reified, and justified in religion, patriarchy and politics, everybody in society is (in)directly linked to the crimes of exploitation. What Kingsolver ultimately targets are the various justifications that we imbue into conceptual distinctions between colonizer and colonized, husband and wife, human and animal, Christian and non-Christian, that allow attitudes of thoughtless violence and unenlightened domination, which as equally describe the sins of European imperialism as an unhappy marital union.

In this way Kingsolver is right to point to her novel as an example of "political allegory" (Meire 83): the story of Nathan Price's family in Kilanga delineates human responses to oppression and unequal treatment as it manifests in all social and cultural guises. As Christopher Douglas points out in the context of the novel's handling of Christian belief, "Kingsolver's . . . critique is that [a] conservative theology of hierarchy and submission—rather than an alternative progressive one of liberation—is toxic in the colonial and neocolonial setting, when invoked, as Belgium and then the US do, to justify paternalism and domination" (136). This paternalism exposes the immoral link between religious rhetoric and colonial ideology, detailing an entire history of exploitation and conquest that has hardly been redressed through more equitable economic policies and the promises of globalization. Elaine Ognibene notes the cynical use of religion by King Leopold of Belgium to continue his pillaging of the Congo: "Leopold used democratic, religious rhetoric to control his rape and pillage of the Congo. . . . Building the infrastructure necessary to 'exploit his colony,' Leopold raised money through the Vatican 'urging the Catholic Church to buy Congo bonds to encourage the spread of Christ's word'" (20). Through Nathan Price's involvement in Kilanga, Kingsolver demonstrates the lingering effects of European and American intervention in Africa in terms of a failed transplantation and translation of beliefs, which in turn unmasks the more selfish motives for their continued presence in the continent. As Leah painfully observes, "by loaning the Congo more than a billion dollars for the power line, the world Export-Import Bank assured a permanent debt that [the country will] repay in cobalt and diamonds from now till the end of time . . . any hope that was left for . . . Independence is handcuffed in debtor's prison" (*PB* 458–59).

Kingsolver's feminist response to this ideological blindness is not to offer yet another conceptual paradigm that holds out an inauthentic vision of utopian politics; instead, she marshals the individual experiences of her female characters (as presented through their narratives) in order to emphasize an alternative orientation toward language that undercuts the false abstractions of imperialist rhetoric. As Anne Salvatore notes, "each woman has a distinct and characteristic way of interpreting the meaning of these experiences," (162) a meaning that cannot be divorced from the bodily marking of trauma. The truth of the female body is thus offered as a corrective against the unthinking intransigence of masculine force. Orleanna trenchantly observes that "to resist occupation, whether you're a nation or merely a woman, you must understand the language of your enemy. *Conquest* and *liberation* and *democracy* and *divorce* are words that mean squat, basically, when you have hungry children and clothes to get out in the line and it looks like rain" (*PB* 383). To destabilize and undermine the masculine grip over conceptual structures is to divest the male speaking voice of any primacy and final legitimacy; as many commentators of the novel have noted, Nathan is himself not accorded any language, his narrative instead being mediated by those he wields patriarchal power over.

What is less commonly observed is how this reversal succeeds in according trauma a central role in the novel's ethical vision. The collective reflections of Orleanna, Leah, and Adah build a portraiture of a man haunted by "a horror too great to speak aloud" (*PB* 196). Nathan's inability to psychologically process "a war injury he doesn't ever talk about" (*PB* 37) emphasizes a vulnerability and loss of control over his masculinity that he tries to compensate for in his tyrannical grip over his family. As Orleanna points out, "he came home [from the war] with a crescent-shaped scar on his temple, seriously weakened vision in his left eye, and a suspicion of his own cowardice from which he could never recover" (*PB* 197): he was the only soldier in his company who survived a death march through his injury and early evacuation. By placing Nathan's actions within a larger context of survivor-guilt that is filtered through the narratives of the characters around him, Kingsolver allows the reader to understand the true extent of his motivations in ways that he cannot allow himself to. Nathan's incomplete handling of his own traumatic experiences is manifested in belated attempts at repression and compensation: just as he fails to see how his repeated forays at proselytizing the natives are in fact displaced efforts at imposing his withered will over his environment, his belief in an implacable God is nothing more than a "posturing desperately beneath the eyes of [a deity] who will not forgive a debt" (*PB* 413). Nathan's death in the jungle, which will not release him from its grasp, accords with his inability to escape from this primal scene of loss; he is denied a future precisely because his ideology cannot allow him a way out of the strictures of "Cowardice, Guilt, and Disgrace" (*PB* 413) that have defined his entire postwar existence.

In contrast to this, Kingsolver suggests that it is the feminine acceptance of vulnerability and pain that allows recognition and responsibility to heal a character's relationship with the past. It is therefore in *living with* guilt and transgression, and understanding our common fragility before it, that we do not become desensitized toward it. Leah voices this truth of Kingsolver as such: "I crave to stop bearing all the wounds of this place on my own narrow body. But I also want to be a person who stays, who goes on feeling anguish where anguish is due" (*PB* 474). In short Kingsolver celebrates a self-reflexivity that is better able to reflect on her language and identity at once conditioned and free, culpable, and capable of redefinition.

Indeed, all of the Price daughters (with the sad exception of Ruth May, killed by a snakebite) are invested in "owning, disowning, recanting, recharting a hateful course of events to make sense of [their] complicity" (*PB* 492), with the attendant hesitations and missteps signaling the difficulty of understanding how forgiveness is possible in the context of an entire history of Western exploitation and damage they feel they are inextricably a part of. However, Kingsolver demonstrates how refashioning is possible as part of the characters' bids for redemption. As with her other novels analyzed in this book, this is actualized in the therapeutic, nonhierarchical encounter between the self and the other, which allows new definitions of selfhood to emerge. In *The Poisonwood Bible* Leah's romantic attachment with Anatole is the catalyst for this change, effectively moving her from passive recipient of Nathan's religious messages to the novel's moral compass. As Kimberly Koza observes, "in a reversal of the colonial view that the colonized have nothing to teach the colonizers, Leah gains wholeness through her love for Anatole, replacing her childhood faith in her father with the political commitment that Anatole symbolizes" (287). Anatole's presence becomes instrumental in decentering Leah's misplaced sense of privilege and moral rectitude, building bridges of empathy between herself and the children of the Kilanga village: "As one girl raised her pounding club the other girl's went down into the narrow hole—up and down, a perfect, even rhythm like the pumping of pistons. I'd watched them time and again, attracted so to that dance of straight backs and muscled black arms. I envied these daughters, who worked together in such perfect synchrony. It's what Adah and I might have felt, if we hadn't gotten all snared in the ropes of guilt and unfair advantage" (*PB* 230).

The abovementioned quote appropriately emphasizes a positive change in perspective: the cultural other is now viewed from a position of plenitude, embodying an unfallen realm of wholeness that exists outside of the political and moral categories foisted upon native bodies by colonial administration. In this moment Leah understands that the Congo belongs to nobody. In a later scene, Anatole challenges her acculturated distinction between Western and African attitudes toward democracy by explaining to her the way of "the native system of government" (*PB* 265). For the Congolese "it seems odd that if one man gets fifty votes and the other gets forty-nine, the first one wins altogether and the second one plumb loses. That means almost half the people will be unhappy" (*PB* 265): instead of clear-cut definitions, they seek compromise and pragmatic arrangements that challenge the separation between the personal and the political.

This process of decentering culminates in an extraordinary passage detailing the beauty and superiority of Congolese civilization, and arts of cultivation, prior to European imperialism, recasting Biblical imagery in terms of an indigenous framework:

> [The Portuguese] reported that the Africans lived like kings, even wearing the fabrics of royalty: velvet, damask, and brocade. Their report was only off by a hair; the Kongo people made remarkable textiles by beating the fibrous bark of certain trees, or weaving thread from the raffia palm. From mahogany and ebony they made sculpture and furnished their homes. They smelted and forged iron ore into weapons, plowshares, flutes, and delicate jewelry. The Portuguese marveled at how efficiently the Kingdom of Kongo collected taxes and assembled its courts and ministries. There was no written language, but an oral tradition so ardent that when the Catholic fathers fixed letters to the words of Kikongo, its poetry and stories poured into print with the force of a flood. (*PB* 520)

Leah's African experience comes to shape her as it (along with the other sensitive female protagonists in Kingsolver) imbues her with new words and concepts to use to describe relationality and belonging. As consonant with what Kathy Weese notes to be a "transculturation process" (9) in the dynamics of Kingsolver's work, this interaction enables difference to positive impact interpretive horizons, drawing out what Kingsolver herself describes as "the places where disparate points of view rub together—the spaces between" (*HT* 154). Just as Leah cannot find the words to depict Georgian agricultural practices to Anatole because of the utter differences in cultural practice, she comes to feel a distrustful distance between herself and Nathan's words, eventually realizing that there are "no real innocents" (*PB* 447) in her country's involvement with Congolese politics. Her final rejection of her father's values is enunciated through a disowning of her homeland, stating that "no homeland I can claim as mine would blow up a struggling, distant country's hydroelectric dams and water pipes, inventing darkness and dysentery in the service of its ideals, and bury mines in every Angolan road that connected food with a hungry child" (*PB* 503).

In contrast to this political awakening, Kingsolver presents a negative picture of accommodation and collaboration in Rachel. Defined completely by vapid capitalist ideals of superficial beauty and American exceptionalism, she contracts a pragmatic marriage to Eeben Axelroot, an unscrupulous merchant who is connected to colonial exploitation via the diamond trade. Rachel's moral blindness is in pointed contrast to her sister's guilt toward American complicity, with the latter noting how Rachel "married a man who may have assisted in [Lumumba's] death-sentence transport to Shaba, though even Rachel will never know that for sure" (*PB* 447). Indeed, Rachel holds on to her racial and cultural difference as a justification to her clinging on to privilege: after managing to move from the Congo to South Africa with her husband, she comments that the locals "will make their houses from a piece of rusted tin or the side of a crate—and leave the writing part on the outside for all to see! But you just have to try to understand they don't have the same ethics as us" (*PB* 424). Rachel thus insulates herself from the traumatic, yet paradoxically transformative, effect that difference brings, instead offering a casual racism that serves to mask her continued reliance on the inequitable dynamics of capitalist economy in order to forge a comfortable and independent existence as owner of the Equatorial hotel.

Her final trust in American pragmatism and individualism, as indexed by her mantra that "you grab whatever looks like it will hold you up" (*PB* 517), emphasizes an unenlightened vision of action unburdened by the historical dimensions of this activity—a cultural amnesia that links Rachel to the collective "unconscious" of her nation. The split between Leah and Rachel implies the dichotomization between remembrance and forgetting that lies at the heart of Kingsolver's politics of the novel: insofar as literary writing can consolidate a dangerous sense of rectitude and superiority that justifies unethical exploitation, it can also be a conduit to amelioration, and a vehicle of self-recovery. Indeed, Kingsolver alerts her reader to the continuing spectral afterlife of Nathan in the context of his children's responses toward the world—one can inherently resist everything he stands for, or one can inherit his values. However, the novel's optimistic vision lies with Leah, who notes how she "loved [her] father too much to escape being molded to at least some part of his vision" (*PB* 504): she recognizes the good intentions that form a part of Nathan's civilizing mission, thereby acknowledging the inevitable "mistakes" (*PB* 533) that arise from this tragic translation of his idealistic visions into reality. In essence Kingsolver does not castigate the ideals that spur men and women into action to change the world; as we have seen in *Animal Dreams*, it is these ideals that mold political consciousness and the desire to preserve and protect a lifeworld. In fact, Leah is ultimately able to balance idealism with awareness about the risks of idealism; she represents a model of commitment that does not shy away from "looking at the truth square on [and] . . . saying it aloud, because it's uncomfortable" (Kingsolver, *SW* 202). In Kingsolver's dialectic there can be no effective action without awareness; by the same token, awareness precipitates committed intervention.

Adah Price's Disability, the Excessive Nature of Language,
and the "Difference" of Translation

Among the Price sisters, Adah occupies a "monstrous" position of liminality, carrying within her body a challenge to heteronormative definitions of disability and inadequacy. Adah's disability, which derives from a hemiplegic condition that affects her mobility and speech, is ambiguously presented as a sign of both deficiency and excess. Her impairment ironically allows her to redefine her identity and wisdom outside of the "myriad of cultural narratives that threaten to 'cripple' her, [enabling her to choose] silence, atheism, and love for her slanted body" (White 132). Indeed, she offers the uniqueness of a poetic consciousness that processes reality through the alternative potentialities offered by literary (trans)figuration. Her language embraces multiplicity and the fluidity of perspectives, eschewing Euclidean space for the "plank clipped into pieces, rectangles and trapezoids" (*PB* 30), which resonates with Kingsolver's overtly postmodern narrative technique of fracturing her tale into the hands of multiple personae.

Through Adah Kingsolver presents a female character who resolutely refuses to be defined and pegged-in by the distinctions between normalcy and disability—she embodies difference *from within* her body. Her status as an outsider paradoxically gives her the power to redefine and reshape language, remaking and destabilizing the assumed finality of Nathan's ideology through creatively deforming it. This is most evidently reflected in her effort to read a book from back-to-front: "When I finish reading a book from front to back, I read it back to front. It is a different book, back to front, and you can learn new things from it. It from things new learn can you and front to back book different a is it?" (*PB* 57). In a novel that consistently emphasizes how truth cannot be separated from the language of its narrator, Kingsolver forces her reader to consider how deforming language and its conceptuality can lead to a new way of understanding reality. For Adah her unique way of inhabiting the world, expressed through her power to reformulate experience to her individuality, incarnates a position of emancipation and productivity.

In a structural way, Kingsolver utilizes Adah's sensibilities to celebrate language's inherent polyphony and heteroglossia. These critical terms derive from the work of the Russian philosopher Mikhail Bakhtin, who argued for a structural understanding of the novel as underpinned by a multiplicity of idiolects and speech acts. For Bakhtin language is always centrifugal in that it constantly decenters itself to embrace multiple sociocultural meanings that link its speakers to a vibrant lifeworld. Because Adah is herself poetically inclined, she is appropriately sensitive toward the heteroglossic register of the Kikongo language, which embraces contradiction and multiplicity: Adah notes at one point that the word "mbote" means "hello and good-bye both" (*PB* 74) in the language. More important, words in Kikongo allow the people who speak it a very different understanding of reality than the Western imagination. As Adah notes,

"*Muntu* is the Congolese word for *man*. Or *people*. But it means more than that. Here in the Congo I am pleased to announce there is no special difference between living people, dead people, children not yet born, and gods—these are all *muntu*" (*PB* 209). Kingsolver once again emphasizes transformative seeing, moments where distinctions framing the Western mind collapse, and an alternative understanding of existentiality becomes possible.

As with the Day of the Dead celebrations in *Animal Dreams*, destabilizing the boundaries between the living and the deceased becomes an important way to return a living consciousness to the natural world (this "spirit" is manifested in the last section of the novel, which is narrated from the perspective of Ruth May), thereby allowing Orleanna a small measure of forgiveness for indirectly causing her death. Indeed, understanding the language enables Adah to transcend her disability, for Kikongo words do not discriminate between "bodies" and the "will" (*PB* 343). In a stark reversal of Biblical imagery, Adah inhabits a prelapsarian realm of perfection in Kilanga, where she is one of "those things perfectly united" (*PB* 343). Indeed, Kingsolver implies that disability and deficiency cannot exist in Kilanga because there is no separation between perfection and deficiency, innocence and evil. Adah's melancholy after leaving Kilanga is therefore in part due to the difference between the "benign approval" (*PB* 72) she is used to in a place where bodies are not subject to medical standards of normalcy, and an America that views the "combination of [a] too-weak body and [an] overstrong will" (*PB* 343) as a monstrosity. In sum living in the Congo frees Adah to be at once ungainly and supple—the homophonic similarity between "*benduka*" and "*bënduka*" (*PB* 493) blurs the distinction between the unsightliness of Adah's gait and the breathtaking flight of the bird. What Adah regards as a source of strength, Nathan treats as an abomination: whereas different meanings from different languages allow her to escape from the strictures of normativity, her father regards linguistic proliferation as another sign of fallenness, a "*Tower of Babel*" (*PB* 168) that must be corrected by reducing received truth to a single belief-system.

It is therefore no accident that Nathan is defeated by a failed act of translation. By appropriating the language of Kilanga to proclaim the gospel, he mistakenly pronounces the word for something "precious and dear" to mean "the poisonwood tree" (*PB* 276). Kingsolver's irony here suggests how the gospel is literally "poison" to Kilanga, decentering a Eurocentric understanding of imperialist rhetoric by playing upon the difficulties inherent in translation. Nathan's attempt at translating the message of God fails precisely because he tries to reduce differences in culture and worldview to an overarching narrative that obviates the specificities involved in this exchange. Where Nathan falls Adah succeeds, because her attention to difference is an authentic trans-lation to the extent that it allows the interaction between the self and the other to increase her interpretive resources. Kingsolver's "postcolonial" novel then forms part of her abiding interest in encountering otherness and translating this otherness as creative difference.

However powerful Kingsolver's moral message presented and sustained in this complex novel is, some critics have accused her of simplifying the real-world politics of postcolonial Congo in the service of simple distinctions between a rapacious West and an objectified Africa. Koza observes that "at times [Kingsolver's] portrayal of the Congo becomes essentialized in the figure of a long-suffering, eternal Africa. . . . Kingsolver's shift to polemic . . . often leads her to generalize, and at times, to oversimplify historical complexities" (288). This criticism is echoed by Stephen Fox, who argues that Kingsolver's representations of the Africans who interact with the Prices "reveal more about [her] own liberal, middle-class desire for political intervention than about the true situation of rural, disabled Congolese" (412). We may go some way toward answering this criticism by insisting that Kingsolver's treatment of otherness aims not so much to romanticize that which is different as it emphasizes how transactions with otherness fundamentally undermine the conceptual frameworks that we put in place to distinguish the self from that which is different from it.

In this reading the "homeliness" of the domestic must become strange *to ourselves,* as otherness decenters cultural privilege toward reimagining what a politics of the "in-between" may look like. As Jacobson writes, Kingsolver performs a "literal unhousing of the protagonist and reader's stable, known sense of the local" ("Imagined Geographies" 182). *Animal Dreams* and *The Poisonwood Bible* both demonstrate how traumatic suffering, and healing from this pain, open up a self that is vulnerable enough to renarrate its relationship with the boundaries that have kept it safe from the impact of ugly, but necessary, truths. An Africa which is hostile enough to wound is also the place that forces the Western imagination to rethink possession, privilege, and historical responsibility, all in the service of getting it better the next time round: "To be here without doing everything wrong requires a new agriculture, a new sort of planning, a new religion" (*PB* 524). Insofar as trauma decenters and dislocates the fixation on the dead present with images of a past that demands reckoning with, it holds out the hope that the future need not be chained to the fatalism of circumstance—what is new is realized as part of a rescripting. With the next two novels analyzed in this book, Kingsolver shifts her attention back to the "local," dealing with fragility once again in the context of the disappearance of an entire "world." The urgency of an awakening needed to fully address the precarity of an ecosystem under threat galvanizes a basic reconsideration of anthropocentric modes of thought—a chance that the abovementioned "newness" may be given a chance to take root within our daily practices.

CHAPTER 4

Symphonic Modes of Understanding in Nature
Prodigal Summer and *Flight Behavior*

The imprint and urgency of Kingsolver's ecological consciousness surface most clearly in *Prodigal Summer* and *Flight Behavior*, novels that are structured on a dialectic between fragile ownership and irrevocable loss. Kingsolver's focus on the importance of a localized sense of place that naturally grounds the individual is as evident in these two novels as it is in *The Bean Trees*, *Pigs in Heaven*, and *Animal Dreams*, but her tone becomes more ambivalent here, juxtaposing her vibrant descriptions of natural life with a didactic prognostication of how this life can be destroyed due to "the cost of [our] various choices" (*PS* 323). The novels set the interactions of their human characters at once in harmony with and at cross-patterns against the natural backdrop of rural Appalachia, while remaining vigilant to the fact that human action can fatefully precipitate momentous shifts in ecological systems whose damage returns us an image of our common vulnerability in the existential sphere now widely given the name "Anthropocene." Using the insights gained from our survey of ecocritical literature in the first chapter of this book allows us to understand Kingsolver's investment in destabilizing the epistemological boundaries between subjective reason and external reality that is offered up as domain to be ordered and manipulated, criticizing our myopic assurance that we are in complete control over the consequences of our actions. In place of this hubris, she recommends watchful circumspection with regards to imbalances and excesses that can cause irreparable damage, the effects of which cannot be fully calibrated.

As Mike Hulme notes, understanding the extent of change that is wrought upon the environment due to human activity involves an almost unimaginable leap of the imagination that severs an image of the future from an empiricism modulated upon the everyday: "human choices five, twenty or fifty years into the future are not predictable in any scientific sense" (83). More than an inert classification and a literary subgenre that brings together works that speak about the "environment," fiction about the Anthropocene enables a critical consciousness that challenges our collective assumptions about technocratic modernity as it impacts a sense of intellectual history and the conceptual paradigms concerning worldhood and embeddedness within that world. What is thereby involved is a substitution of unpredictability for certainty—Kingsolver's enmeshment of her human characters within natural systems that are "a grand sight more complicated than we like to let on" (*PS* 216) powerfully suggests how the notion of individual choice is both illusory and necessary, stemming both from a "participation in biological systems . . . within and outside of [ourselves]" (Leder 230) and a cognizance that each choice creates "a world made new by the chosen" (*PS* 1).

As we have seen with her other novels, Kingsolver returns obsessively to the philosophical notion that concrete human action and responsibility effectively intervene in defining futural possibilities. The novels about climate change and environmental impact allow her to press home the political urgency of acting to forestall a global catastrophe from which nobody can escape. Kingsolver sounds an apocalyptic note through direct imagery in her essay "Setting Free the Crabs," where she states that "there must be limits, somewhere, to the human footprint on this earth. When the whole of the world is reduced to nothing but human product, we will have lost the map that can show us how we got here, and can offer us our spirits an answer when we ask why" (*SW* 72). In response to anthropogenic commodification, Kingsolver uses her fiction to enunciate a vital sense of the "open," a realm resistant to objectification and crisscrossed by planetary flows in excess to the narrowly human.

Kingsolver's concern with the utter obliteration of a shared history with nonhuman others not only espouses an "ethically driven reconceptualization of human responsibility in our relationships to [these] life forms," but also invites reflection upon the political claims of this tenuous control that we have over the world in our desire for knowledge (Yang 76). Insofar as human action results in unforeseen consequences that transcend the "localized," they bring into play scalar effects that disrupt binaries between nature and culture, or what Timothy Morton has pithily called an idea of the world. As he writes, "there is no background, and thus there is no foreground. It is the end of the world, since worlds depend on backgrounds and foregrounds. *World* is a fragile aesthetic effect around which we are beginning to see" (99): nature is the *only* frame through which we see anything at all. This encompassing instability suggests that the world that we have inherited is the only world that we have and that we can lose—it has an agency that we must engage with, and that we must be accountable for. The existential thrust of this statement is made clear by Frederick Buell, who states that climate change and global warming presents the "consummate natural-cultural crisis, today an inside without an outside, without alternative or way back or clear path forward" (270). As these two novels demonstrate, the urgent work of science, which resolutely reckons with "evidence [that] will keep coming in" (*FB* 506), is hampered by communal skepticism and narrow economic self-interest, forces which must be continually corrected.

Indeed, it is the courage to look things squarely in the face that Kingsolver admires in the scientific method. As she states in her novel *Unsheltered*, "in science, we are constrained by cause and effect. We collect data and examine it. We're allowed to use nothing outside of the evidence to make our explanations" (*U* 335). However, as *Flight Behavior* and *Unsheltered* also show, information can be politicized and wielded to serve divergent ideological ends. Kingsolver's response to this pessimism necessitates a productive bridging of the illusory gap between nature and culture: her fiction attempts to resituate knowledge about the environment from being, in the words of Timothy Clark, "only a passive ground, context and resource for human society" toward "an imponderable agency that must somehow be taken into account of, even if we are unsure how" ("Climate-Change" 134). In other words the difficulty facing Kingsolver's characters is how to chart a path into the future where all "was impermanent. . . . This one little life signified nothing in the long run; it would get eaten" (*FB* 577). In contrast to Taylor Greer's narrative of initially yearning for flight and escape only to become more rooted to a new-found sense of belonging, these two novels present characters who learn how tenuous ownership over a place ultimately is.

In this way both *Prodigal Summer* and *Flight Behavior* demonstrate how knowledge about place, and the need to protect and preserve a living and dynamic relationality to the notion of place, is deeply organic. It breaks down anthropocentric ideas about privilege and ownership in order to reconstitute concepts of autonomy and self-understanding on the basis of a sense of responsibility that is owed to the future as chance and crisis. Just as we "share the object of [our] live[s] with whole communities of the dead" (*PS* 76), we are entrusted with the thoughtful stewardship of the earth's resources for the unborn. Kingsolver's fictions about climate crisis are therefore balanced on a knife-edge between collapse and rebirth; they demonstrate Sylvia Mayer's arguments about climate change novels being risk narratives, wherein the "awareness of the impossibility to fully account for 'side-effects' that come with complex technologies and their applications [as pertains to environmental harm] always implicates a certain degree of non-knowing" (208). What I will emphasize is how Kingsolver employs this element of "non-knowing" not only to decenter the anthropocentric focus on knowledge to allow alternative, affective modes of relationality to become essential tools to understanding but also to re-turn to human action as having a proper moral dimension we require in order to change the image of the present.

Being and Belonging in *Prodigal Summer*'s Radicalization of Innocence

Reflecting about *Prodigal Summer*, Kingsolver notes her aim to unsettle anthropocentric readerly frameworks that prioritize individualistic struggle and transcendence over circumstances rather than a thoughtful circumspection on the ecology of existence, a mindset that productively breaks down barriers between nature and culture, human and animal. In this mode of thinking about relationality and codependence, human activity is at once beholden to a non-human materiality that precedes the scope of our volitions and empowered to meliorate the future totality of environmental wordhood. As Kingsolver states, the novel solicits "a broader grasp of connections and interdependencies than is usual in our culture" (qtd. in Leder 227): what is required is an interpretive effort that replaces "linear, binary grids of logic and reading" with "complex, overlapping systems of entangled matter and meaning" (Meillon 62). While cognizant of the limitations of this approach (in terms of our desire to ground readerly interest in human characters and their interactions with other characters), an ecocritical understanding of the novel succeeds in destabilizing the distinctions between characters as subjective bearers of value and nature as mute, objective background, so as to accord the sense of place with aesthetic value in terms of how landscape carries with it the burden of memory and the problematic idea of management that involves stakeholders from different strata of society.

Far from it being an unapproachable realm of the Sublime in Romantic poetics, or an inauthentic commodification of unfallen innocence that we either despoil or escape into, Kingsolver refines her understanding of Zebulon County as a nexus that is "produced through situated histories involving the politics of material production and accounts of environmental change" (Jenkins 36): place squarely *exceeds* the boundaries between nature and culture, objective fact and emotive value, thereby troubling our desire to consign it to a passive witness of the vicissitudes of history. Indeed, Kingsolver is determined to destabilize the very paratextual semiotics that privilege anthropocentric reference over the dynamic unfolding of nature as a prodigal, excessive text: her sections of the novel are titled "Predators," "Moth Love," and "Old Chestnuts," signifiers that remove indications of human characters while also defining the main sources of conflict that structure her three novelistic set-pieces. "Predators" is mainly focalized through Deanna Wolfe, a woman who works as a ranger preserving the coyote population in the forested areas of Zebulon County. "Moth Love" is told through the perspective of Lusa Maluf Landowski, a disaffected entomologist of Polish heritage who must negotiate both the management of her family farm after her husband Cole Widener unexpectedly passes away, and the conflicted relationship that she shares with her husband's extended family. "Old Chestnuts" humorously details the antagonistic struggles between Garnett Walker, a widower who is neighbors with a feisty apple farmer Nannie Rawley. Their clashes over the use of pesticides give Kingsolver the space to fold in ideological debates between evolutionism and creationism with the development of a grudging respect between Garnett and Nannie. This evinces Kingsolver's interest in negotiation and conciliation over the blind imposition of a theoretical framework that is insensitive to the interfacing that occurs between materiality and conceptuality, ideas about place and the place of an idea within an unfolding multiplicity.

In line with her emphasis on systematicity in place over epistemological distinctions between nature and that which is excluded from it, these "interwoven" stories accrue their own time-space specificity, while pointing to the fact that each story unfolds within a shared openness of landscape that is subtly changed by the actions and decisions taken by any one of the characters. In this way the aesthetic structure of *Prodigal Summer* registers how the "relationships between the manifest human and natural worlds are constantly being reconstructed, restructured, and newly imagined" (Narduzzi 63).

"Predators" reimagines embodiment and belonging in terms of Deanna's sexual awakening. Through her liaison with a young hunter, Eddie Bondo, Kingsolver overturns our inherited distinctions between innocence and corruption, human sociality and creaturely desire by observing how nature is itself suffused by a creative and (re)generative spirit that can reclaim a deeper sense of belonging to a community. In this way Kingsolver allows nature to "'talk back' and 'punch back' at humans" (Yang 77), not in an antagonistic way, but in a fashion that foregrounds correlation and symphonic understanding. Kingsolver's technique thereby enables a double consciousness, an artistic vision that sets the unfolding of the human drama of her characters alongside "a consciousness that pauses, observes, and records as if in a scientist's notebook" (Wagner-Martin, *Barbara Kingsolver's World* 127). This happy marrying of the language of the scientist and the language of the novelist suitably troubles the distinction between observation and evaluation, reimagining nature as abundant partner to more authentic modes of self-understanding. Deanna's sexual awakening can be seen as a powerful rescripting of the Judeo-Christian narrative of mankind's fall into corruption and original sin, where Eve is positioned as a passive vessel of gullibility and temptation. As Kingsolver sees it, Deanna's sexuality is at one with nature's excess, overflowing heteronormative understandings of desire with an originary innocence that can remake the world again:

> The dawn chorus was a whistling roar by now, the sound of a thousand males calling out love to a thousand silent females ready to choose and make the world new. It was nothing but heady cacophony unless you paid attention to the individual entries: a rose-breasted grosbeak with his sweet, complicated little sonnet; a vireo with his repetitious bursts of eighth notes and triplets. And then came the wood thrush, with his tone poem of a birdsong. The wood thrush defined these woods for Deanna, providing background music for her thoughts and naming her place in the forest. (*PS* 52–53)

As this passage details, a keen sense of observation is allied to a sensorial multiplicity that increases a sensitivity to *other*ed modes of belonging to the world. In other words Kingsolver's language attempts to bridge the gap between anthropocentric language and that which lies in excess of it: the artistic complexity represented by the "sonnet" and the "bursts of eighth notes and triplets" sustains a chorus that must be approached and understood via what ecocritic Laurence Buell describes as a "capacity . . . to awake[n] to fuller apprehension of physical environment and one's dependence on it" (22). Kingsolver's artistic strategy here cannot be reduced to an uncritical romanticization of nature as unfallen realm of fullness; instead, this performance of sexual desire and fecundity that cuts across human and nonhuman agents invalidates and reorientates the distinctions between thinking and feeling, being-with and belonging-to. In the words of Suzanne W. Jones, "in an attempt to disrupt an anthropocentric world view, Kingsolver personifies animals and animalizes people" (93); this sentiment is demonstrated clearly when Deanna senses that she is "like some fresh animal born with its own volition" (*PS* 20) through her attraction toward Eddie.

In this way Kingsolver succeeds in reclaiming an Edenic space that does not seek so much to return humanity back to a state of prelapsarian innocence, as to renegotiate the very terms through which the primal unity between human beings and nature can function as symbolic fiction and utopian ideal. The novel's focus on strong female characters who combine the careful attention to detail and observation of a scientist with an idealistic impulse to refashion a better world by altering inherited practices of pesticide use, tobacco-farming, and unsustainable hunting practices thereby maintains a clear ecofeminist stance, wherein the "meld[ing of] scientific and experiential epistemologies" (Houser 96) emphasizes how effective intervention must be situated from within a holistic understanding of ecological systems that function on disparate and heterogenous scales. Deanna espouses this organic form of knowledge in her constant exhortations to Eddie that "removing a predator has bigger consequences for a system" (*PS* 319), urging him to consider the incalculable effects of altering an element in an entire ecosystem. As Yang puts it, ecofeminism is not so much another absolutist ideological framework that replaces extractive economy, but a way of thinking about the costs of intervention "that challenge[s] hierarchical and categorical segregations of humans, nonhuman animals, and the environment to introduce more dialogical configurations of the various active agentic matters interdependently coexisting in this planet" (76).

This theoretical inflection on Kingsolver's interest in ecology posits that it is the creative and ethical potentialities of difference that properly suggests ways in which modes of thought can be challenged and destabilized—in this context, it is relationality thought about differently that changes collective attitudes toward nonhuman others that present alternative ways of thinking about personal identity and kinship structures. Just as the reconstituted families in *The Bean Trees* and *Pigs in Heaven* provide a changed outlook on familial responsibility and political citizenship, the uncanny resonances between humans and animals in *Prodigal Summer* sustain both a thinking of commonality, and a hearkening toward our shared fragility in the context of an ecosystem on the verge of utter destruction: Deanna bemoans the fact that she "didn't make up the principles of ecology" (*PS* 179), thereby implying how every action is calibrated to either destroy our communal heritage or to carry "the hope of something wondrous in the making" (*PS* 204).

What Kingsolver therefore makes us feel is the necessity of preserving difference as it pertains to alternative visions of how "humans think about their *place* in the world's ecological systems" (Van Tassel 91). As Deanna reflects about her mission to protect the coyote population, Kingsolver outlines how the coyote family substitutes maternal care and sustenance for patriarchal domination as such: "Everything that was possible to know about them, though, Deanna knew. That only the alpha female would bear young, for instance; the other adults in the pack would forego reproduction. They'd support the alpha instead, gathering food, guarding the den, playing with the pups, training them to forage and hunt after they emerged with their eyes open. If their parents got killed, the pups would hardly suffer for their absence—that was the nature of a coyote family" (*PS* 57). Deanna's intellectual knowledge about the coyotes suitably combines with a gradual affective openness to the natural rhythms of the embodied experience in order to suggest how she carries within her the seeds of a momentous change that opens up onto a future only ever intimated within the pages of the novel, a future symbolized by the child she bears with Eddie who returns her to the claims of human sociality and responsibility.

This importance placed on Deanna's procreative capabilities accords well with Greta Gaard and Patrick Murphy's argument that ecofeminist texts posit the female body as "sites where . . . transformations can continuously occur" (9): Deanna's understanding about the coyotes holds out the promise that kinship structures, which have been traditionally been associated with patriarchal imbalances that feed into masculine attitudes of dominance and objectification, can be ethically reimagined alongside larger projects of reconceptualizing the future of ecological belonging. As the sections of the novel dealing with Lusa will demonstrate, Kingsolver is as much concerned with loss as well as rebirth: if our place in the world is irrevocably altered through human action, then old ways and attitudes of relationality can cede in favor of more egalitarian ones. Just as Deanna comes to understand that "she would never again be herself" (*PS* 434) through the giving of her entire self in union with Eddie, Lusa's story revisits the experience of trauma as outlined by characters in her earlier novels while depicting the process of rebirth as willing participation in the unfolding relationship between human characters and their landscape.

Lusa's Regeneration and the Intertwining of History with Landscape

Kingsolver forges convergences between Deanna's narrative and Lusa's, demonstrating how her characters are organically linked to a blossoming into a fuller definition of community, one that articulates its possibilities in tandem with natural cycles of decay and regeneration. For Amanda Cockrell, the link that connects all organisms as parts of a developing ecosystem is sexual attraction; as she writes, the novel "is about sex: people sex, bug sex, coyote sex; about pheromones and full moons, and the drive to pass on your genes. . . . Sex is urgent and dangerous, to the human heart as well as to the lacewing" (188). Deanna and Lusa's sexuality are worked out at the edges between human custom and natural abundance; the latter's erotic attractiveness solicits unwanted attention from members of her extended family, including her nephew. As with the powerful depictions of "courtship and mating" (*PS* 52) around her that Deanna senses, Lusa ponders connections between the mating patterns of moths that she studies, and her own situation. Kingsolver strikes a more somber note with Lusa's narrative to act as counterpoint against Deanna's, for her gradual reawakening into a changed identity (as symbolized by the adoption of the Widener name) is hard won in the face of much "loss and mourning" (Narduzzi 61), which ultimately makes her transformation that much more affecting for the reader.

Already feeling suffocated in a marriage with Cole that narrows down her existential options and stymies her idealism within the confines of a rural environment, Lusa ponders how she and Cole "were a biological cliché . . . [of] a male and female following their separate natures" (PS 35). Driven by her education to regard natural organisms as precious and worthy of respect and conservation, she is dismayed to be living "with these people who seemed determined to exterminate every living thing in sight" (PS 32), with the utter mismatch between her ideals and her social environment leading to fractious conversations and disagreements with Cole. Her alienation is compounded by the difficult relationship she shares with Cole's extended family, which comprises his four sisters who are presented as insensitive and meddling. Their collective distrust against her emerges most clearly in their suspicions that she is eyeing the family plot of land that she will inherit. Lusa's racial heritage as a half Polish, half Palestinian Jew squarely positions her as the threatening outsider, one whose transnational identity is at first presented to be disadvantageous in terms of her integration into her environment. Lusa's vulnerability is then ultimately compounded by the untimely death of Cole in a truck accident; she searches in vain for something "to hold her in this place" (PS 239). As with Kingsolver's other female characters who deal with traumatic memories and life events, the failure to synthesize and integrate the present with the past further entrenches them in misery, as they lack the perspective to narrate their experiences as part of a meaningful trajectory.

The challenge for Lusa, as outlined by Kingsolver, is to arrive at a vantage point wherein "her marriage would someday be fully apparent to her memory's eye and yet untouchable" (PS 303); this working-through occurs as she gradually reaches a deeper understanding about the bonds that connect her with the farm she takes responsibility for. This ultimately implies that Lusa is no longer trapped and beholden to the past; she can change her family's futural relationality to the land by adopting "a practical and responsible approach to land use—one that accounts for the fact that humans are active participants in and members of their ecosystem, not separate from it" (McConnell and Saladyga 34). In a word, the fact that ecosystems are dynamic (and not static entities to be manipulated) suggests that human practices can shape better futures, just as they are shaped and changed by processes that remain open and contingent.

It is therefore fitting that Lusa's intimations of the processes of natural regeneration, at a level that transcends the conceptual edifice of language, draw her back into "the world's trust" (PS 413) and allow her to transcend her negative fixations upon loss. Kingsolver foregrounds the significance of sensorial immersion as a way the world's immanence imprints itself upon consciousness, emphasizing a "biocentric engaging with the world that relies on intuition and uninhabited perceptions" (Meillon 77): "but there were so many other things besides words. There were the odors of honeysuckle and freshly turned earth, and ancient songs played out on the roof by the rain" (*PS* 239). Kingsolver thereby reflects Clark's argument that acknowledging and being receptive to the imponderable agency of nature productively decenters anthropocentric ways of separating subjective reason from objective backdrop, allowing new ways of understanding environmental totality to emerge. Kingsolver's context for this in *Prodigal Summer* is noticeably erotic; both Deanna and Lusa are profoundly affected by a nonhuman experience of *jouissance* (or affective desire that erupts in excess of linguistic representation), which opens up their bodies to the fullness of encounter and union with an otherness.

Kingsolver punctuates this via a surreal dream of sexual copulation that Lusa has concerning a moth-like being whose presence precisely troubles the distinction between human and animal:

> He was covered in fur, not a man at all but a mountain with the silky, pale-green extremities and maroon shoulders of a luna moth. He wrapped her in his softness, touched her face with what seemed to be the movement of trees. His odor was of water over stones and the musk of decaying leaves, a wild, sweet aura that drove her to a madness of pure want. She pushed herself down against the whole length of him, rubbing his stippled body like a forest between her legs, craving to dissolve her need inside the confidence of his embrace. (*PS* 79)

The powerful eroticism of this passage not only breaks down the barriers between reason and passion ("a madness of pure want"), but also encodes feminine sexuality as pure excess that dissolves the dyads human/animal, nature/culture, transgressing these boundaries so as to change the conceptual frameworks through which they operate in our symbolic totality. Indeed, inasmuch as the feminine in Kingsolver's novel deconstructs the opposition between innocence and corruption, it also substitutes a radical becoming— a dissolution of stable identity—for enduring being. In other words, Kingsolver privileges process over finality, echoing the philosophers Gilles Deleuze and Felix Guattari's arguments that the human being is only ever in-process of becoming animal: anthropomorphic identities are always in a state of flux, never becoming settled and stable. Kingsolver's most radical presentation of this idea manifests itself in the becoming-animal of Lusa; she senses how she awakens other human-animals who/that are being drawn to her scent: "Now after years spent suppressed in hibernation, her ovaries were waking up and kicking in. No wonder the men were fluttering around her like moths: she was fertile. Lusa let out a rueful laugh at life's ridiculous persistence. She must be trailing pheromones" (*PS* 230).

As with Kingsolver's use of simile elsewhere, the notion that her suitors are being compared to moths does not reductively collapse the difference between human behavior and animal instinct; instead, difference defines alternative ways we conceptualize our positionality within a strange and frequently surprising ecosystem. At the same time, Lusa's dominance as moth queen resists patriarchal objectification and subjugation; she is primed to reconstitute the Widener family's relationship to their land by taking advantage of her knowledge and experience of local conditions. In short Lusa's reawakening is as much sexual as it is intellectual; observation is happily married to experiential immersion in an environment she takes on as responsibility toward the future.

What Lusa ultimately comes to embrace is the fact that inheritance has to negotiate with the ghostly dimensions of the past. In this view the natural landscape is never a neutral, inert realm that offers itself up as unlimited resource; instead, taking care of the land you have been entrusted with comes with a responsibility to steward a spatial repository of memory, regret, and lost futures. Lusa herself reflects on the uncanniness of sharing "the objects of your life with whole communities of the dead and never give them a thought until one of your own crossed over" (*PS* 76); through Cole's death, Lusa intuits that she is indelibly connected with past generations who have tended the land. What an ecocritical perspective adds to this evocation of historical haunting is the fact that we owe a debt of responsibility to the multitude of nonhuman beings whose narratives have also been etched onto the landscape—a reminder of our shared heritage with other lives and narratives. Kingsolver thereby balances elegiac remembrance with the hope that human agency can redress inequality and offer new ways of thinking about responsibility. Deanna thus mourns the animal species that have gone extinct, thereby losing a world: "So many others never would rise again: Bachman's warbler, passenger pigeon, Carolina parakeet, Flint's stonefly, Apamea moth—so many extinct creatures moved through the leaves just outside her peripheral vision" (*PS* 59–60). By bearing witness to the ghosts of the past through commemorating them in language, Kingsolver suggests that we become more mindful of the consequences of our unthinking actions that have deprived them of a future.

At the same time, the "ghosts" that Lusa inherits—family heritage, received farming wisdom, patriarchal conventions—need not prevent her from changing these ossified practices for the better. Alistair Fraser has correctly pointed out how the reliance on tobacco farming for the Wideners demonstrates how "rural space . . . [intersects with] the logic of capital accumulation" (147), leading to a nuanced examination of how economic necessity often mitigates against systemic change. However, Lusa represents a happy rapprochement, for her turn toward utilizing the land for goat farming turns out to be both ecologically sustainable and profitable. Drawing upon her heritage and knowledge of Jewish and Muslim customs, her choice of rearing goats for food instead of tobacco emphasizes how "economic and environmental success" (Wenz 117) is both possible and desirable. Once again Kingsolver's focus on determined and informed action that is cognizant of practical necessity while also being driven by idealistic aims does offer a form of resistance against the stranglehold of capitalist logic.

To reiterate Kingsolver's point, it is only by viewing the relationships between living beings in terms of systems and interconnections that we become more aware that every decision we make is a decision for the future—it changes and remakes the world differently. As Katherine Thiele argues, the image of the world shifts from a static backdrop that needs to be managed at a distance toward an "intra-active place 'on' which worlding *matters* at every moment" (211). Kingsolver's ecofeminist sensibility thereby alters the final image of the hero from that of a masculine conqueror who masters the forces of nature to that of a committed individual who finds herself "married to a piece of land named Widener" (*PS* 383), the image of union foregrounding a shared partnership between human needs and conversation of the biosphere. Just as Kingsolver rescripts the cultural image of Eden in order to restructure the relationality between human beings and the natural world, she presents an alternative vision of resurrection, where Lusa's "progress toward understanding" (*PS* 437) results in a rebirth *from within* this world: not transcendence from the phenomenal world, but the transformation of the everyday. Kingsolver's handling of the dialogue between religion and science emerges most clearly in the sections involving Garnett and Nannie, and it is this note of openness that works to bridge what are commonly held to be antagonistic explanatory systems of thought.

Science and Religion as Dialogic Partners in Kingsolver

Kingsolver's own training as a biologist allows her a familiarity with certain scientific concepts that she clothes in artistic fashion so as to give dramatic weight to these ideas in the *specific contexts* of her characters' situations. Speaking about the writing process behind *Prodigal Summer*, Kingsolver realizes the difficulties involved in translating these scientific concepts in ways that would seem organic to the development of a plot worthy of readerly interest, while recognizing the necessity of raising the level of ecological consciousness via the fictional medium:

> I wanted to write a novel to bridge th[e] gulf [between art and science]
> somehow. Specifically, I wished I could explain a handful of important eco-
> logical principles: speciation and natural selection, the keystone predator,
> genetic diversity and resilience, and the Volterra principle, which (for in-
> stance) shows mathematically why spraying a field with pesticides actually
> will increase the number of pests in the next generation. These principles
> profoundly shape the world around us, in which we hope to survive. . . .
> Translating scientific ideas from clean, elegant mathematics into vernacular
> English was a huge challenge. It's easy to oversimplify or alter meaning
> (qtd. in Wagner-Martin, *Barbara Kingsolver's World* 118).

One of the evident aims of *Prodigal Summer* is pedagogic; Kingsolver wants to
turn our attentions to the "detail [that] goes unnoticed in the world" (*PS* 170),
for careful observation of the ways in which natural systems persevere, correct,
and maintain themselves inculcates respect for the complexity of physical and
biological laws.

In the context of the novel, Kingsolver positions scientific knowledge as a
corrective against shallow cultural depictions of animals that mitigate against
proper ecological understanding. As Deanna muses, the antagonism that
human beings feel against coyotes, thereby making them view the animals as
nothing more than fearsome predators to be eliminated, is falsely perpetuated
through cultural stereotypes that succeed in demonizing them: "The farmers
she'd grown up among would sooner kill a coyote than learn to pronounce
its name. It was a dread built into human via centuries of fairy tales: give man
the run of a place, and he will clear it of wolves and bears" (*PS* 28). Part of
what makes the relationship between Deanna and Eddie a mutually sustaining one is that as he awakens her to the benefits of human companionship,
she in turn educates him on the need to preserve the coyote population as part
of a healthy ecosystem with a dominant predator. Kingsolver is then clearly
optimistic that scientific knowledge, when combined with the "innate human
desire to draw closer to living things, to 'gasp' in sheer delight" (Hanson 260),
can productively change sedimented attitudes toward questionable human
practices.

However, Kingsolver does regrettably come across as heavy-handed and
preachy in her use of female characters as vessels of ecological wisdom. Nannie's role in the novel is clearly a foil for Garnett's close-mindedness; she offers
the reasonableness of the scientific perspective to counterpoint against his dogmatic adherence to creationism. At one points Kingsolver has Nannie unsubtly
explain the Volterra principle to her neighbor as if she is reciting this truth
from a textbook on ecological principles:

"All right. When you spray a field with a broad-spectrum insecticide like Sevin, you kill the pest bugs *and* the predator bugs, bang. If the predators and prey are balanced out to start with, and they both get knocked back the same amount, then the pests that survive will *increase* after the spraying, fast, because most of their enemies have just disappeared. And the predators will *decrease* because they've lost most of their food supply. So in the lag between sprayings, you end up boosting the numbers of the bugs you don't want and wiping out the ones you need. And every time you spray, it gets worse."

"And then?" Garnett asked, concentrating on this.

She looked at him. "And that's it, I'm done. The Volterra principle." (*PS* 275)

The character dynamic between Garnett and Nannie provides an interesting tonal variation on the novel's other male-female interactions, for Kingsolver seems to be more concerned here with the ideological contention between religion and science, than deep character development on the level of Lusa, or even Deanna. In fact, Kingsolver loads the dice unfavorably against Garnett: as an older character who espouses antiquated views about women and who is noticeably xenophobic against Mexican immigrants, his views never carry significant moral weight as against Nannie's. Indeed, Garnett's reliance on religious doctrine to provide an overarching explanation for a chestnut blight that robs his family of their traditional means of subsistence classifies him as a character (together with the members of Dellarobia's community in *Flight Behavior*) who mitigates against the evidential, rationalistic approach that the scientific method exemplifies. This division unequivocally emerges in the language both use via letters to each other that challenge ideological assumptions and viewpoints. Garnett's adoption of a Christian mindset unfavorably privileges anthropocentric dominance, terms that ultimately justify his use of pesticides:

Are we humans to think of ourselves merely as one species among many, as you always insist in our discussions of how a person might live in "harmony" with "nature" while still managing to keep the Japanese beetles from entirely destroying his trees? Do you believe a human holds no more special authority in this world than, say, a Japanese beetle or a salamander? If so, then why is it our duty to set free the salamander, any more than it is the salamander's place to swim up to the state prison in Marion and liberate the criminals incarcerated there? (*PS* 186)

Garnett's unthinking citation of Genesis obviates any further critical debate; his appeal to authority is clearly shown to be laughably limited and myopic.

What Nannie offers in rebuttal is a decentering of perspective, a viewpoint that challenges any claim that human beings are accorded centrality and mastery in the context of what Karen Barad calls "the open-ended becoming of the world" (182). As Nannie writes back to Garnett,

> I do believe that humankind holds a special place in the world. It's the same place held by a mockingbird, in his opinion, and a salamander in whatever he has that resembles a mind of his own. Every creature alive believes this: The center of everything is *me*. Every life has own kind of worship, I think, but do you think a salamander is worshipping some God that looks like a big two-legged man? Go on! To him, a man's a shadowy nuisance (if anything) compared to the sacred business of finding food and a mate and making progeny to rule the mud for all times. (*PS* 215)

Once again Kingsolver's unequivocal adoption of an ecofeminist stance tips the debate in favor of characters who maintain the interconnectivity between the human and nonhuman aspects of ecology; they turn vulnerability into existential resource, urging us to both think into the positionality of nonhuman beings, and to think with entities and systems that lie beyond our control, manipulation, and understanding. Garnett's ideological position on the stability of God's creation is thereby shown to be untenable, as he "does what [he does] claiming not to believe in the very thing he's done" (*PS* 279), crossbreeding the American chestnut with the Chinese to survive a future blight. The novel's celebration of diversity cuts across the human and the biotic: just as Lusa embodies the positive complexity of her transnational heritage and racial identity, even using it to benefit her family, an ethical relationality toward the land and its use combines economic necessity with ecological care. For Kingsolver it is the conversation between art and science that both concretizes abstract geological and biological principles, and allows literary endeavor to be about this world—the novelist and the scientist can meet in the space hollowed out by common questions about worldhood and affective belonging to this world.

While I cannot agree with Richard Magee's observation that Garnett and Nannie's exchanges "challenge the simple dichotomy of science and religion" (74) due to Kingsolver's almost didactic stance on the necessity of scientific inquiry, I maintain, together with McConnell and Saladyga, that the novel's championing of diversity enacts a theoretical focus on conversation, troubling clear-cut binaries in order to allow us "to think about the ways that different values can co-exist and inform one another" (28). As much as Kingsolver understands the scientific perspective to be a valuable guide toward knowing our place within ecological totality, she also implies that this knowledge needs to be shared and embraced amicably among neighbors who need to come together to make things better. Nannie's wisdom is thus not an imperious imposition of her ways of doing things onto Garnett; she acknowledges that she needs to work with him to solve their common problems of pest management and collective stewardship of the land they share. Her efforts of conciliation serve to build rapport with Garnett, allowing her a glimpse into his vulnerabilities stemming from the early death of his wife and disappointment about his son. If, for Kingsolver, all art is political in that it offers a vision of how "the possibility of a kinder future" (*SW* 264) can be realized, then it embraces abstract ideas and concepts as much as the sense of the everyday, and how that everyday can be shaped by thoughtful reconsideration of practices involving consumption and production. As Fraser notes, "acting locally cannot only mean acting alongside others in a locality but also that there are real gains to be made from trying to change those in close, close proximity. Opposing and subverting dominant processes and actors shaping the contemporary global politics of the rural entails this horizontal act of speaking to those in close proximity, especially because their precise proximity provides scope to communicate and speak" (148).

As Kingsolver sees it, to speak effectively is to sustain dialogue between different agential players whose unique contributions all add a piece to a vast tapestry crossing history, politics, and art. It is this image that Lusa draws upon in her final meditation on natural beneficence: "this was the Tree of Life her ancestors had woven into their rugs and tapestries, persistently, through all their woes and losses" (*PS* 383). Within the ambit of this dialogue, science and religion can now be regarded not so much as antagonistic explanatory systems, but rather symbiotic endeavors that invoke a sense of reverence and awe toward the mystery of creation and life. Indeed, Nannie drives home this point in her appeal to Garnett's religious sensibilities, writing that "I'm partial to the Genesis you quoted, but I wonder whether if you really understand it. God gave us every herb-bearing seed, it says, and every tree in which is the fruit of a tree-yielding seed. He gave us the mystery of a world that can re-create itself again and again" (*PS* 217). Seen in its proper perspective, the abundance of the natural realm locates the transcendent within the quotidian; the insights attained through scientific inquiry cannot be a value-neutral pursuit after objectifiable data that reduces reality to a "project" to be managed but must change attitudes and practices that prioritize the unlimited expansion of human desires in a disenchanted world without any barriers to this growth.

In other words, what science and religion properly inculcate in us in the notion that nature is radically "other" to us, forever in excess to our constructions, a break in our notion of "reality" that registers in the mode of the apocalyptic. As queer ecologist Catriona Sandilands writes, nature is "an unrepresentable kernel around which discourse circulates but which language can never fully apprehend" (203). Kingsolver's employment of religious imagery in *Prodigal Summer* and *Flight Behavior* precisely gestures toward this break in conceptual representations of worldhood that reenchant the space of the everyday. However, if the emphasis in *Prodigal Summer* is on regeneration and rebirth, a resurrection into "new life" (*PS* 439) wherein the innocence of primeval creation can be experienced again, *Flight Behavior*'s mode is starkly apocalyptic. Kingsolver grimly raises the stake for action against the backdrop of the loss of an entire world, a situation from which there is no escape whatsoever. In such a risk-laden world where the tipping point between present and future, maintenance and collapse is unknowable, Kingsolver equates the birth-into-consciousness of Dellarobia with a continual intimation of crisis, wherein every action has momentous consequences on a personal as well as on a global scale. In short Dellarobia's awakening is the precipitation of the political.

Risk, Crisis, and the Burden of Revelation as Dellarobia's Mental Frameworks

Kingsolver's novel attempts to both present the impossibility of maintaining the political status quo in the context of a world that is about to be radically altered through anthropogenic activity reaching a threshold point, and to imagine the conditions for "an alternative to the present" (*FB* 56), which precipitates in an awareness of crisis that shifts our basis sense of spatiality and temporality. In an 2012 interview on the novel, Kingsolver clearly foregrounds how her fiction cannot ethically indulge in escapist constructions that promise us the world will continue functioning the way it has if we continue to live the way we always have; instead, her writing must rupture the very foundations of our ideological coordinates and puncture these symbolic fictions, thereby demonstrating that to be "insecure and . . . desperate" (*FB* 130) defines the existential *topoi* of a global community who can envisage no other way out of a crisis situation. As she says, "We don't see the effects of climate change, we don't see that melting sea ice. It's hard for us to believe that the world under our feet could ever be any different than how it's always been. I think the human animal has a fundamental trust in certain kinds of continuity. It's hard to convince ourselves that that's not the case. But most of all we're wired to fight or flee. That's the title of the novel. It's *Flight Behavior*. Every cell in our body wants to run away from the big scary thing" (qtd. in Wagner-Martin, *Barbara Kingsolver's World* 197).

In a stroke Kingsolver argues for fiction's capacity to press home the urgency of seeing truth for the uncomfortable entity it is and explains our in-built avoidance to facing these truths: "flight behavior" is as much biological as it is psychological. The growing sense of dread at what the displaced monarch butterflies represent is balanced alongside depictions of inertia, fueled by fantasies of escape that mitigate against effective political intervention because they "promise to enable business-as-usual to continue, whether psychological, economic, or ecological" (Murphy 159). Indeed, Dellarobia's awareness of the untenability of life as it is lived under present conditions precipitates in an ethical vision of crisis and responsibility toward the future as both chance and possibility that the present can be altered. As she muses about her son's place within a world that could be inevitably disappearing, she feels "an entirely new form of panic . . . wondering if he might be racing towards a future like some complicated sand castle that was crumbling under the tide" (*FB* 341). Dellarobia's image of collapse not only resonates with a generalized condition of loss that threatens civilization at its very core, but also opens up a critical perspective toward the possibility of the unimaginable that radically exceeds linguistic and conceptual framing—ecological destruction alters the very means through which we represent time as existential coordinate. Kingsolver's aim is thus placed firmly in terms of a responsibility we owe toward others who will inherit the world entrusted to us: as she notes about her novel, depicting the preciousness of the environment in need of care and conservation signals "our obligation . . . to the people who aren't born yet" (qtd. in Haynes 131).

As Kingsolver sees it, the unique difficulty facing the literary representation of the effects of climate change is that it demands the making-visible of the invisible, or the registering of catastrophe within the logic of the present. Environmental collapse is therefore a concept of the concept-less; it radically modulates the Kantian notion of the Sublime to emphasize the breakdown of representational modes in the face of an event that may have already happened within our symbolic universes. In the words of Dale Jamieson, the utter failure to imagine what comes *after* environmental collapse "reflects the impoverishment of our systems of practical reason . . . and the limits of our cognitive and affective abilities" (178)—we run up against an impenetrable barrier against any existential projection of human possibility from the present into the future. It is worthwhile to revisit Mayer's arguments about risk: what such a situation problematizes are modernist concepts of subjectivity, technology, and political organization that sustain us in an unbroken narrative of continuity. What risk tells us is the utter provisionality of all projections; "what is important is not logic based on former periodicities, but multiple projections from present imbalances" (Buell 277).

Imbalance is thereby the only appropriate starting point of *Flight Behavior*; Dellarobia Turnbow is determined to "come loose from [her] station in life" (*FB* 7) by running away and having an affair with a stranger. She is prevented from doing so by the almost unearthly sight of the monarch butterflies who have sustained an unnatural migratory journey due to changes in weather patterns. It becomes crucial to Kingsolver's message that the presence of the butterflies register themselves onto Dellarobia's consciousness at a level prior to that of logic, for they represent a complete break within the symbolic edifices that she tries to escape from. In other words, they call her back to a life that now demands to be negotiated via alternative lenses and means:

> She was on her own here, staring at glowing trees. Fascination curled itself around her fright. This was no forest fire. She was pressed by the quiet elation of escape and knowing better and seeing straight through to the back of herself, in solitude. She couldn't remember when she'd had room for being. This was not just another fake thing in her life's cheap chain of events, leading up to this day of sneaking around in someone's thrown-away boots. Here that ended. Unearthly beauty had appeared to her, a vision of glory to stop her in the road. For her alone these orange boughs lifted, these long shadows became a brightness rising. It looked like the inside of joy, if a person could see that. A valley of lights, an ethereal wind. It had to mean something. (*FB* 21)

Kingsolver's evocative language in this passage (and in others describing the sensorial impact of the butterflies) preserves the biblical meaning of "apocalyptic" as "revelation": Dellarobia thinks she has been "called out to witness" (*FB* 30) an event that transforms her life. Kingsolver plays with the literary conventions of self-discovery as reflected in the genre of the *Bildungsroman*, for Dellarobia's seeing "straight through to the back of herself" (*FB* 21) does not come about through the conquering of external circumstances, but through the empathetic sharing of vulnerability and loss that links her fate to that of the butterflies. In a poignant reformulation of the masculine narratives of Jack London and Ernest Hemingway that set into conflict "Man against Nature" (*FB* 339), Dellarobia understands that the otherness of nature shows up the very limitations of patriarchal attitudes of dominance and exploitation. Consonant with Kingsolver's presentation of other female characters who succeed in a working-through of traumatic experiences, it is the recognition of fragility that allows the self's relationship to language and reality to be changed for the better—Dellarobia intuits the unnatural presence of the butterflies as an unsymbolizable "wounding" in the ecosystem, a gaping chasm that returns an image of damage she is emotionally drawn toward. Dellarobia's understanding of the significance of the butterflies' migration as "a truth she could feel" (*FB* 315) usefully particularizes and concretizes the hard truths of climate change into personal experiences of change and loss.

It is therefore in Dellarobia's apocalypse that Kingsolver marries the intellectual and affective dimensions of awakening; through Dellarobia, Kingsolver allows her reader to both "understand and *feel* the magnitude of the potential consequences and risks we are both creating and taking" (von Mossner 130) through anthropogenic actions, the effects of which are imprinted upon vulnerable bodies. Dellarobia's rebirth into critical consciousness positions her outside of the frames of reference that circumscribe her class and gendered consciousness; through her, Kingsolver implies that it is possible to engender change from within a particular mode of life. In this way Dellarobia's narrative is indeed an "ecocritical" one insofar as the critical provenance of the term highlights a paradigmatic shift from accustomed ways of relating to the world; it recenters "utopian" consciousness from an other-worldly realm to a changed understanding of what the here-and-now can be.

In a word this consciousness is both critical and re-mediative, positioning human actions and decisions as momentously instrumental in shaping a future as the chance for living under different conditions. Kingsolver thereby agrees with the idea that responsibility is genuine and authentic only when it is unprogrammable, when it carries within itself the unforeseeable nature of risk; in this way, the knowledge of the "Anthropocene" carries with it both disaster and utopian possibility. As Rebecca Evans argues, the conceptual estrangement performed by ecological reframing shows us a "new world" that is different from "the familiar [one in that] the integration into the past and the future of that which capitalist logics have always ignored [is made central to the salvation of this world]: the insistent presence of costs that were never in fact external to a global system, and the animacy of nonhuman and multispecies systems such that "nature" is not inert, but is dynamic in a way that can produce radically disjunctive environmental futures" (485).

To be sure, Kingsolver does not hesitate to present the structural limitations to concerted action against environmental destruction: the inequities of outcomes due to class stratification, and the lack of economic options that define a negative relationality toward the land as exploitable resource, are acutely realized in Dellarobia's family who resist her exhortations against selling their allotment to a lumber company for clear-cutting. Dellarobia's tragedy is partly defined by the fact that her life-altering vision of the butterflies is a sight and "knowledge [which] was hers alone" (*FB* 60), for she cannot share the full significance of this harbinger of catastrophe with anybody around her. As Kingsolver depicts it, the other members of her family are occupied with justifiable economic concerns that mitigate against conservation of the forest: her husband Cub is weighed down with keeping the finances of the family afloat due the uncertainties of his occupation, and her father-in-law Bear has to figure out a way to settle his loans for farming equipment which have been rendered virtually unusable due to inclement weather partly caused by climate change. A significant portion of Kingsolver's novel is thereby dominated with the struggles between Dellarobia's increasingly strident advocacy of the need "to open our eyes and have a look before we stated logging up there," (*FB* 97) and the undeniable fact that "a logging contract was money in the bank" (*FB* 111)—resistance to understanding and acting against climate change is premised both on the notion that "no one has actually lived through a climate apocalypse" (Rosenthal 275–76) and that a commitment to environmental action is usually associated with certain socioeconomic privileges which avail conservation as an option.

Once again Kingsolver emphasizes how thinking solely in terms of large abstractions entrenches an undesirable idealism that fails to consider the specific barriers and impediments toward meliorative societal change. The novel's synthesis between the global effects of anthropogenic climate change and the specific, affective dimensions of Dellarobia's elegiac mourning for the "impermanence" (*FB* 577) of all biotic life-forms denotes a positive consideration of the absolutely unpredictable scalar effects of seemingly unremarkable events that resonate with other events in ways that exceed and defeat representation. In the words of Ursula K. Heise, "climate change poses a challenge for narrative and lyrical forms that have conventionally focused above all on individual, families, or nations, since it requires the articulation of connections between events at vastly different scales" (205). As Kingsolver modulates Heise in her novel, raising collective awareness of this connectivity requires a critical perspective that is at once sensitive to the disjunct between the "hard-core science about planetary vulnerability and . . . the lived experience of limited material resources" (Rosenthal 278) and idealistic enough to think out of the existential conditions imposed upon us by capitalist logic.

Flight Behavior demonstrates how consciousness of ecological crisis can serve to provide an alternative to capitalist exploitation. As Christopher Lloyd and Jessica Rapson point out, "the novel urges us to see ourselves within a planetary perspective without leaving our very human, localized attachments" (913). Dellarobia's sense of crisis that "the butterflies were a symptom of vast biological malignancies" (*FB* 531) cannot be separated from her awareness that this is a world that is about to be lost for her children—it is paradoxically "the great slog of effort that tied up people like her in the day-to-day" (*FB* 320) that enriches her consciousness of place as an open interface between localized networks of significance and the larger imperatives of ecological justice. This connection ties her narrative with other stories of displacement and loss, not only with reference to the butterflies that have arrived from Michoacán, but also with a Mexican family she encounters who have lost the means of their livelihoods together with the animals' migration. The importance of the local, and the value of wonderment at the miraculous display of a natural realm both resilient and fragile, raises objects in that realm above commodification, returning an unalienated unity between the human being and his or her environment that resists the imposition of disenchanted value within a capitalist world order. Indeed, as Naomi Klein observes, "climate is about an early blooming of a particular flower, an unusually thin layer of ice on a lake, the late arrival of a migratory bird—noticing these small changes requires the kind of communion that comes from knowing a place deeply, not just as scenery but as sustenance" (158–59).

For Kingsolver the embeddedness of knowledge within a particular locale changes attitudes of exploitation and dominance to that of wise stewardship. Dellarobia's understanding of the butterflies is religious to the extent that it incarnates an awareness of the totality of the environment as *other*worldly, or that which is radically other to anthropocentric frameworks: "miracle or not, this thing on the mountain was a gift" (*FB* 139) entrusted into her care. To reiterate, the conceptual notion of the gift ruptures relationships based on symmetry and commensurability, for it suggests an excessive givenness and presence that cannot be exchanged or reciprocated. This presence, as pure qualitative difference from commodification, thereby situates consciousness as vigilance over the consequences of our actions, for it raises the question of how we are to relate to, and indeed, care for, objects outside of their use and exchange value. For Kingsolver the intersectionality between ecological consciousness, scientific inquiry, and existential practice is what allows action to have positive social and political significance. As she observes in her essay "The Memory Place," "Poverty rarely brings out the most generous human impulses, especially when it comes to environmental matters. Ask a hungry West African about the evils of deforestation, or an unemployed Oregon logger about the endangered spotted owl, and you'll get just about the same answer: I can't afford to think about that right now. Environmentalists must make the case that we can't afford *not* to think about that right now" (*HT* 174).

Indeed, Kingsolver draws attention to the ways in which environmental consciousness can function as the spur toward reimagining the basis of human community. Dellarobia's poignant image of catastrophe *from which there is no escape* not only foregrounds the desperate need for remediation that must be enacted in the present, but also implies the falsity of a futural denouement that is premised upon the modality of the present: "In one transcendent moment buoyed by about two ounces of Riesling she saw the pointlessness of clinging to that life raft, that hooray-we-are-saved conviction of having already come through the stupid parts, to arrive at the current enlightenment. The hard part is letting go, she could see that. There is no life raft; you're just freaking swimming all the time" (*FB* 543). Dellarobia's pointed use of the term "enlightenment" provides a staunch critique of enlightenment values of reason and transcendence over natural being, attitudes that have come together to shape an untenable future based on subjective domination over nature.

However, as I have argued earlier, the negative image of crisis is precisely u-topic as opportunity to shift the symbolic coordinates of reality. In other words being conscious that there is only ever constant "swimming" to be done precipitates action as having unlimited political significance: the personal is nothing less than the political. As with *Prodigal Summer*, Kingsolver reiterates her message that it is choice—to be kinder, more loving, and ethically responsible—as reflected in the everyday that changes the world as totality of those choices. It is therefore the opportunities afforded by working toward environmental justice that show Dellarobia how "man [can] ever be *for* anything" (*FB* 183): If we are to avert the coming disaster, it is imperative that we renegotiate all our attitudinal stances toward the world. The ecological crisis then might become a way that our symbolic structures are helpfully exposed as fictions that can be substituted for better ones. Dellarobia thereby becomes the conduit through which divergent modes of inquiry may be reconciled; she unites theoretical knowledge with practical awareness, adumbrating an understanding of the world which is changed not by a hierarchical imposition of ideas, but by an organic belonging to the conditions of class membership that crucially does not preclude a standing-apart from these conditions. Kingsolver's dialectical conception of knowledge and action is presented via Dellarobia's interactions with the scientist Ovid Byron.

Dellarobia as Organic Intellectual and the Dialectical Synthesis between Knowledge and Action

As we have seen, the raising of Dellarobia's consciousness betokens a politicization of knowledge, presented as an awareness of the need for immediate action that changes the ways in which we live our lives. It also argues for a positive dialectic between knowledge and action: theoretical concepts lose their efficacy to motivate and inspire change and existential practice if they are severed from contexts of daily application. By the same token, action needs to be informed by understanding that brings with it a proper perspective. Kingsolver's resistance to postmodern relativism and skepticism is demonstrated through her insistence that the science behind climate change is nonnegotiable; it is the frame around which we need to reorganize our politics and economics. Indeed, Kingsolver is not only interested in making scientific concepts relevant and accessible via the fictional medium, but also endeavors to demonstrate how "a common language" (*FB* 209) between people from different class and racial backgrounds is possible.

Kingsolver's presentation of knowledge is thus a nondesiccated form of inquiry, one that unites awareness of planetary fragility with the human motivation to act. This perspective is much needed in the world of *Flight Behavior*, which shows the reader how people still "differ radically as they attempt to discern *what* [factual information about climate change] means" (Wagner-Martin, *Barbara Kingsolver's World* 11); interpretation is still required to set knowledge in its appropriate context. Dellarobia gloomily discerns how the information provided by an informed scientist such as Ovid will still fail to galvanize economic practice in her locale, Feathertown, not because there is too little information, but ironically because there is too much: "Nobody truly decided for themselves. There was too much information. What they actually did was scope around, decide who was looking out for their clan, and sign on the memos on a wide array of topics" (*FB* 228). The resistance to committed action required to halt environmental damage comes about through collective denial and the need to define "survival in their own terms" (*FB* 543), thus rendering knowledge as something which entrenches divisions, rather than playing a unificatory and liberatory function.

In the context of Dellarobia's family, the blindness toward evidence of climate change is positioned as an economic one as much as an ideological one: the deep-seated Southern religious beliefs of her in-laws results in a dimmed perspective that suggests "the Lord moves in mysterious ways" (*FB* 204), negating further examination of natural phenomena in favor of trust in Providence. As Kingsolver analyses it, a further sign of the domination of a capitalist system is its separation between knowledge and practice. Insofar as "ecological consciousness" and the information required to make sense of complex scientific data about climatology and animal behavior (together with the resources supporting this knowledge) is concentrated in the hands of the intelligentsia, this knowledge proves to be ineffectual to alter the ways in which the capitalist mode of production has penetrated the lives of people who have few options outside of treating the land as economic resource. As Dellarobia herself muses, "there were two worlds here, behaving as if their own was all that mattered" (*FB* 209). Synthesizing a critique of class relations with ecocriticism is therefore to imply that "inequalities, alienation, and violence inscribed in modernity's strategic relations of power and production" (Moore 170) become inscribed in arguments about the full historical impact of the "Anthropocene." Bringing a critical sensibility to bear upon the intersections between production, consumption, and ecology enables Kingsolver to nuance the terms of the debate: if ecological awareness is to effect a paradigm shift in political economy, it must organically raise class consciousness so as to bring attention to the "diminished social and environmental conditions" (Houser 107) that mutually reinforce the working class's oppression and disenfranchisement, and ultimate resistance to changing the status quo. In other words ecological consciousness must powerfully bring across the idea that present conditions have become unequivocally untenable and unsustainable.

Dellarobia thus functions as a character best suited to precipitate an awareness of crisis, for like the butterflies, her fate is uncertain by the end of the novel. Dellarobia's need to escape and to find a new life away from domestic confinements is powerfully paralleled to that of the butterflies, which tragically fail to flourish in their new environment. The emotive appeal of Dellarobia's narrative resonates with the reader's sympathies for the butterflies, resulting in a blurring of "the lines between environmental and domestic politics, converging the romance plots with their environmental messages" (Jacobson 8). Dellarobia's growing sexual attraction to Ovid (which ultimately remains unrealized) emerges alongside her informal "education" in climate science: as we have seen with other Kingsolver characters, the feminine is the site where radical transformation becomes possible, where the porous boundaries between desire and intellect challenge the patriarchal separation of mind from body. Kingsolver's ecofeminist leanings go one step further, for she is able to understand the affective deficiencies present in Ovid's dispassionate reliance on hard evidence in order to change mindsets. Ovid's single-minded focus on the merits of observation and measurement ironically ensconces him in an ivory-tower of knowledge that has not been dialecticized with meaningful action; as Dellarobia senses, "people who'd never known the like of Ovid Byron would naturally mistrust him" (*FB* 356).

Dellarobia thus understands that "the task of science was a good deal larger than that" (*FB* 337), for it must go beyond the value-neutral appearance that Ovid presents it as in order to perform a proper hermeneutic role of explaining and altering the human being's relationship to his or her environment. Indeed, what Dellarobia offers is a feminist epistemology, a way of embedding information within the sphere of the everyday; in opposition to the separation between subjective reason and objective reality that the scientific method instantiates, a conceptual connectivity that bridges knowledge and action, thought and emotion. As with other female characters in Kingsolver who succeed in modulating masculine attitudes, Dellarobia manages to shift Ovid's tunnel vision by sensitizing him to the class-bound impediments to lifestyle changes in response to information. In fact, she alerts Ovid to the notion that positionality within intellectual debates between the economy and the environment enables a helpful scrutiny of the complex interactions between class privilege, ecological justice, and political consciousness:

"Information is all we have." Ovid stared back at her, somehow managing to look as naked as she'd ever seen him. Which was very. "Everybody chooses," he said. "A person can face up to a difficult truth, or run away from it."

She shook her head. "My husband is not a coward. I've seen him stick his whole arm into the baling machine to untangle the twine while it's running. Trying to save a hay crop with rain coming in. I mean, if we're talking guts. He and my in-laws face down hard luck six days a week, and on Sundays they go pray for the truly beleaguered."

He seemed to take this in, even though he probably didn't know as many men as she did who'd lost am arm to a baling machine. "These positions get assigned to people," she said. "If you'd been called the bad girl all your life, you figure you're already paying the price, you should go on and use the ticket. If I'm the redneck in the pickup, fine, let me just go burn up some gas." (*FB* 445)

Dellarobia's strident tone turns her class limitations into a form of strength, as she is able to articulate the need for knowledge and information to be particularized in order to respond to her experience of the lived reality of the people around her. At the same time, Kingsolver emphasizes how her assistance with Ovid's scientific research affords her the perspective from which to transcend the narrowness of her class concerns toward a critical reframing of her mode of existence. It is thereby in Dellarobia that Kingsolver effects the desirable synthesis between theoretical and experiential capacities, intimating how the production of knowledge can emancipate the oppressed by returning them an image of their own transformed capabilities outside of economic systems of disempowerment and restrictions. However, this possibility is at best envisioned beyond the pages of the novel—Kingsolver's emphasis on the uncertainties of future life in a world about to change irrevocably leads her to imply that Dellarobia might not be able to escape completely from her life to find "a new earth" (*FB* 597). Instead, the novel places its trust in the future, as represented by Dellarobia's children Preston and Cordelia. They are at once a powerful reminder of the ecological responsibility the present generation owes toward future ones, and the hope that awareness of the temporal rupture between the shape of the present and the shape of the future is both the risk of collapse and the opportunity for radical change: "Despite everything, the end of the world impending, Dellarobia had a glimpse of strange fortune. . . . A whole melting world surrounded them. She noticed Preston's eyes wandering back to their house, and could read his thoughts like a book: Mom, Dad, apartment, etcetera, all starting to sink in. The loss or rearrangement of everything he's ever known and trusted" (*FB* 590).

This chapter has considered the alternative reimagining of temporality, politics, and economics under the pressures of ecological crisis. As Kingsolver argues for in her writing, what considerations of environmental catastrophe allow us to do is to reevaluate the significance of human action as something that fundamentally changes the potentialities for future generations to have a world—in this respect, human responsibility has never mattered more. At the same time, the risk of climate apocalypse destabilizes the idea that we can carry on the way we have always done, enabling a perspective that reads signs for radical shifts and displacements, rather than continuity and homogenous perdurance. In a word Kingsolver is interested in reading narrative differently, not as another instantiation of an abstract metahistorical theory, but as a de-centered universe of shifting possibilities. Indeed, this consciousness allows us to, in the words of Greg Garrard, "look back upon ourselves today with a sense of shame and embarrassment" (qtd. in Lloyd and Rapson 925) that our ideals and rhetoric have passed over silences and gaps that fiction can reimagine and bring to life. These alternative narratives feed into Kingsolver's ethical interest in historical fiction, which is at one with her larger project of decentralizing accepted political truths.

CHAPTER 5

Filling in the Gaps
The Lacuna and *Unsheltered*

Kingsolver's interest in historical crises as refracting our contemporary political situation powerfully informs her aesthetic design in *The Lacuna* and *Unsheltered*. Both novels recognize the intellectual and scientific developments that have pushed society forward and the benighted forces threatening to retard this development. Although *The Lacuna* and *Unsheltered* may not seem to involve themselves with ecocritical themes, I extend the theoretical insights of ecofeminism to the dimensions of feminist historiography. Insofar as ecofeminist insight unearths a different understanding of the human being–nature connection through an appropriation of masculine discourse, feminist historiography aims to uncover the anonymous contributions of women to the shaping of knowledge. *Unsheltered* undertakes the narrative work of imagining the forgotten life of Mary Treat, an unconventional spirit "free to examine the world as she saw it" (*U* 229), thereby participating in the labor of historians who have documented the scientific activities of various women in the sixteenth and seventeenth centuries (Park 143). As I will analyze, a feminist practice of writing history concerns itself with narrativizing the gaps left out in the official account of things past—this aesthetic informs *The Lacuna*'s emphasis that "the most important part of the story is the piece of it you don't know" (*L* 652).

For Kingsolver, applying the lenses of historical analysis to unpacking our ingrained resistance toward difference as it manifests within political rhetoric not only allows us to chart wider cultural movements that reflect the contemporary with respect to regrettable legacies of oppression and discrimination, but also endows us with the critical capacities to think this history differently. In her essay "Jabberwocky," Kingsolver juxtaposes media sensationalism with historical analysis, arguing how the "information that corroborates a certain narrow view of the world and our place in it" feeds into a prepackaged presentation of moral and political self-righteousness that obviates a wider understanding of our historical responsibility toward those we have silenced through fear and intellectual obtuseness (*HT* 226). As she elaborates, "the safest marketing technique is to dispense with historical analysis, accountability, and even—apparently—critical thought" (*HT* 226–27). In turning toward an altered image of history that relentlessly punctures holes in an untroubled narrative of patriotism and self-determination, Kingsolver aligns her art with political critique, utilizing larger patterns of significance to investigate the ways in which "a large part of America is uncomfortable with challenging the *status quo*" (Holmquist 1). This interest is as much determined by Kingsolver's emphasis on reimagining the cultural environment within which these entrenched ideas stymy genuine political debate as it is by destabilizing the representational frameworks that inform historiography. On a more personal note, these novels form part of a writerly response to the vitriol Kingsolver received as one of the few people who publicly criticized America's invasion of Iraq after the events of 9/11. In a word *The Lacuna* and *Unsheltered* are thinly veiled attacks on the status quo.

As much as her novels fit into the paradigms of contemporary literary criticism, Kingsolver contributes to the corpus of works scholars have classified as historiographical metafiction. Practiced in the context of a postmodern understanding of history, which seeks to dismantle the hermeneutical primacy of any one overarching narrative, these literary texts locate and celebrate "inevitable contradictions and multiplicities in the historical record" (Tolan 288), thereby demonstrating how every "narrative representation—storytelling—is a historical and political act" (Hutcheon 51) that foregrounds notions of order and comprehensibility as an attempt to synthesize meaning and consequence from the messiness of lived reality. Historiographical metafiction involves a double scrutiny of history and narrative, highlighting how the judicious selection and arrangement of events turns existential occurrence into a momentous turning point, character into an agent of change. As the historian Hayden White points out, "all historical narratives contain an irreducible and inexpungeable element of interpretation" (51): the act of storytelling forms an important part of our cultural need to understand the present in terms of our past, and to discern an intelligible directionality that imbues our current actions with larger significance. As Kingsolver herself details, our sense of history enables us to fit these trends into a useful perspective that retrieves ways of negotiating crisis and loss of certainty: "There's no recipe for how to fix an economic collapse and climate crisis. Our news media don't always help, when they flood us with superficial glimpses of disaster, or lurid gossip about people we will never meet. It's not surprising that readers may be hungry to put our experience into a more useful context. . . . Historical fiction can be a part of that" (qtd. in Wagner-Martin, *Barbara Kingsolver's World* 173). The sense of history can provide comfort by placing struggle and the threat of collapse within larger sweeps of time whose meaning can be usefully activated by retelling this story again.

However, Kingsolver's abiding investment in difference implies that she approaches historical fiction with a feminist sensibility. By probing the ways in which historical narrative is a project as much informed by a thrust toward greater understanding and clarification as it is about creatively transforming "the missing page [and] void" (*L* 464), Kingsolver emphasizes how a feminist rewriting of history seizes upon the necessary gaps within the official record to alter our relationship with it. Situating Kingsolver's novels with respect to a feminist practice of historiography signals that we "approach history as a malleable, physical body of knowledge to be re-visioned, re-cited and re-worked continually into new narrative forms" (Horne 50). Comparing *The Lacuna* with *Unsheltered* reveals how Kingsolver rescripts historical events not only to retrieve the monumental efforts of women who anonymously contribute toward advances in scientific understanding, but also to disrupt the hegemonic patriarchal narrative of American exceptionalism. This disruption is crucial in that it allows a critical perspective that resists the intolerance and bigotry against those members of the community who have been "othered" and silenced due to their difference from the status quo. As Carrie Rentschler and Samantha Thrift argue, a feminist practice "can cut across dominant ways of narrating history as a series of hyper-visible turning points by developing new ways of thinking about temporality, social transformation, and expressions and practices of dissent, and in doing so, help produce new contexts for political and cultural practice" (241). Once again for Kingsolver, difference becomes important in allowing us to have a transformed relationality to our historical selves; as the forward-looking biologist Mary Treat argues in *Unsheltered*, "when the nuisance of old mythologies falls away from us, we may see with new eyes" (*U* 89).

In examining Kingsolver's feminist historiographical method as practice, I focus on its techniques not so much as part of a monolithic ideology as a "strategically adopted political position from which to write" (Horne and Tobin 76); her method challenges dominant paradigms in order to "redress narrative perspectives that previously privileged male-centered and male-authored versions of history" (Muller 22). To put it differently, if the dominant patriarchal historiographical paradigm emphasizes closure and unidirectionality, then a feminist practice unlocks this certitude in favor of the potential to disturb and unsettle. As we will see, Kingsolver leverages gaps—across space and time—to suggest how the historical sense of ourselves is always *in process*. This sensibility accords well with the philosopher Claire Colebrook's arguments about the feminist mode of temporality, which continually takes up the problematics of selfhood as constructed at a variance from history. As she elaborates, "if we are beings who exist through the sense we make of ourselves, we are also beings whose narrative materials, whose past and archive, are not exhausted by the uses we make of them" (13). Historical determinism is thereby blasted open by "the wide-open moment" (*L* 408) of difference, which solicits us to take up its meaning in a utopian fashion (as changed understanding of what the present can be). Kingsolver's metafictional gestures probe the indeterminacies that become endemic to any construction of the past at the same time as they suggest how "there is room for imagining the role of judgment, dissent, difference, and change—*within* community" (Romano 472).

Versions of History and Selfhood in *The Lacuna*'s Emphasis on Absence

Kingsolver's longest novel functions as oblique commentary upon the vitriol visited upon her by the media after her controversial comments in the wake of the 9/11 attacks. Clair Sheehan outlines how Kingsolver's atypical response to America's "war of terror" casted her as a pariah:

> In many outspoken, pre-9/11 essays and op-ed articles, Kingsolver criticized America's involvement in the Middle East and Persian Gulf, questioning the primary motivations behind US actions there. For this reason she was better placed than many of her fellows to argue convincingly when politicians appeared to exploit the 9/11 tragedy, using it as justification for a headlong rush into another war. Previously Kingsolver's criticism and liberal opinions had been met with little significant censure. When she began to decry the jingoistic rhetoric to be heard and read in the news coverage that followed the attacks, however, her words met with much harsher judgment than had hitherto greeted them. (196)

Kingsolver is clear that her criticism against unthinking jingoism and discriminatory political rhetoric does not amount to a wholesale rejection of patriotic ideals. In her essay "And Our Flag Was Still There," she writes that "questioning our government's actions does not violate the principles of liberty, equality, and freedom of speech; it exercises them" (*SW* 242). As she passionately argues for earlier in the essay, the need for critical awareness and civic tolerance becomes increasingly important in the face of extreme right-wing opinions that ferment in the wake of such a tragedy, viewpoints that threaten the very foundations of democracy. Kingsolver rejects a "brand of patriotism [that] specifically blamed homosexuals, feminists, and the American Civil Liberties Union for the horrors of September 11. . . . [These] hoodlum-Americans were asking me to believe that their flag stood for intimidation, censorship, violence, bigotry, sexism, homophobia" (*SW* 237–38). As if writing in direct response to this knee-jerk reaction against heteronormative constructions of American citizenry, Kingsolver focalizes her novel through Harrison Shepherd, a homosexual writer whose dealings with Leo Trotsky, Frida Kahlo, and Diego Rivera in the turbulent years leading up to WWII land him in trouble with the House Committee on Un-American Activities (HUAC) under Joseph McCarthy.

Kingsolver's turn toward historical fiction is as much concerned with problems of its narrativization as it is with a misremembering of history: repetition serves as a cautionary reminder of the similarities between the persecution of suspected Communists in the McCarthy period and the contemporary situation following 9/11. Read as an allegory of the American political landscape following 9/11, Kingsolver adroitly collocates "the politics of mass hysteria around McCarthyism" with "the manufactured fear that drives the so-called war on terror" (Seaboyer 136), using her fiction for strident political commentary in ways that advocate for complexity and nuance in relation to the collective awareness of the country's past. As Shepherd himself comments, "most of [the public] don't know what communism is, could not pick it out of a lineup. They only know what *anti*communism is" (*L* 493). Retrieving a different account of history then becomes important for Kingsolver to unsettle the ideological certainties that serve to reify false moral absolutes. Indeed, it is the easy absorption of political rhetoric that allows America to have an untroubled relationship with its past; as Kingsolver analyzes it, this unawareness about historical violence and oppression is politically expedient when easy distinctions between aggressor and victim enable American citizens to "subordinate [themselves] to the national good" (*L* 377).

Kingsolver's novel is political to the extent that it places the history of America under scrutiny, arguing for what Liesl Schillinger (in a review of *The Lacuna*) calls "conscience and connection" (2) across historical time periods. This metahistorical consciousness surfaces via a conversation between Shepherd and his secretary (and eventual archivist) Violet Brown, emphasizing the need for a reckoning with the past that dispenses with easy answers and solutions in favor of acknowledging how political identity is constructed based on a misrecognition of historical culpability against those who do not conform to the status quo:

> "Mr Shepherd, you do not. But some do. They look around and say, 'This here is good, and that is evil,' and it's decided. We are America, so that over there must be something else altogether."

Mrs. Brown will never cease to amaze. "That's very insightful. You think that comes of cutting our anchor to the past?"

"I do. Because if you had to go sit on a grave and think hard about it, you couldn't just say, 'This is America.' Some Indian would cross your mind, some fellow that shot his arrow on that very spot. Or the man that shot the Indian, or whipped his slaves or hung up some tart woman for a witch. You couldn't just say it's all fine and dandy." (L 531)

It is thus Kingsolver's historiographical method that fashions an aesthetic around gaps and holes in the record. These gaps offer relevant political commentary insofar as they suggest how "the most important part of any story is the missing piece" (L 364): history is a narrative that must be understood differently *from itself* if it is to allow us better ways of understanding our present circumstances. As organizing principle the lacuna signifies both the silences of Shepherd's life that must be rescued from oblivion and narrativized if that life is to bear "honest witness" (L 664), and the gaps in historical understanding that crucially reimagine the foundational truths of a polity. Markku Lehtimäki correctly observes that the novel is "teeming . . . with numerous textual practices . . . rather romantically implying that journalistic or political discourse is bleak and empty when compared to the interweaving of narrative modes made possible by literary art" (130). What is needed to supplement this critical insight is how this layering adumbrates an *othered* approach to narrative and history that suggests the truth of the historical and political self is always in process. In other words reading the gap *as* gap allows us the critical space through which to reassess historical circumstance so as to understand how it "cleaves and for one helpless moment stands still . . . the two halves rest on end, waiting to fall" (L 392)—the shape of history has the potentiality to be different from itself.

The Lacuna is therefore a novel suffused with liminality and transitional spaces: as the young Shepherd shuttles his way back and forth between Mexico and America, he "begins the process of navigating his identities" (Boyles 196) as provisional and always in the process of becoming. Compositionally the "narrative" is a mixture of newspaper reportage, letters, and disparate segments of Shepherd's life that serve to mediate the reader's access to the "historical" personae within the novel. Kingsolver adds in the figure of Violet, whose shaping hand is metafictionally presented in sections of the novel titled "Archivist's Note." Beyond the (by now) familiar postmodern point that all stories are inevitably mediated by conventions of storytelling and narratorial perspective, Kingsolver harnesses the compositional ethos of incompletion to emphasize how the genre of historical fiction incarnates an ethical dimension of reimagining the relationship between the personal and the public. To return to my argument about the relevance of feminist historiography to the novel, Kingsolver employs a feminist sensibility in order to represent "a research and composing practice that utilizes aggregated layers to construct a multivocal narrative about the past" (Wetzel 14). This multiplicity generates active forms of engagement with the past not only to upset certainties, but also to suggest how the very incomplete nature of the historical record implies that we can retrieve forgotten possibilities and redress historical injustice.

In the context of the novel, Shepherd's literary productions about the "history" of ancient Mexico are attempts to creatively renegotiate the ideological impact of colonialist narratives about Spain. Kingsolver pointedly employs the metaphor of the lacuna as it pertains to the ancient people of Mexico who have been forever lost to history; as Frida Kahlo notes, "the people of Teotihuacán had no written language . . . we can't read their diaries . . . or the angry letters they sent their unfaithful lovers. They died without telling us their complaints" (*L* 261). This gap in the historical record implies that the history of Mexico is inevitably mediated by their colonial conquerors: Kingsolver ironically details how the two books on the Aztecs consists of "all of the letters written by Hernán Cortés to Queen Juana of Spain, who sent him off to conquer Mexico" (*L* 69). This rewriting of history from the perspective of the victor has ideological consequences for societal attitudes toward the marginalized; Kingsolver demonstrates this through presenting how the young Shepherd imbibes a simplistic story of Spanish benevolence toward the violent Qualpopoca, which serves to legitimize colonial brutality and conquest by force: "The Azteca in other cities were not so friendly to the Spaniards, and killed them. One was a big troublemaker, Qualpopoca. Cortés demanded him brought in for punishment, and to be safe decided to put Moctezuma in chains, but on a friendly basis. Qualpopoca arrived fuming, insisting he was a vassal of no Great King from anywhere, and hated all Spaniards. So he was burned alive in the public square" (*L* 71).

In this way *The Lacuna* not only reflects the contemporary politics of America through a collocation of historical events, but also refracts humanity's regrettable tendencies toward xenophobia and identity politics through the Spanish conquest of Mexico, followed by America's anti-Japanese sentiment against her own citizens during the war. This sentiment is captured by the irrational fear stoked by the mass media against the Japanese beetle, which (as construed by *Life* magazine) threatens to overwhelm agriculture: "The beetles, however, are firmly settled on our middle Atlantic coast, where they chew up apples, peaches, grapes, roses, pasture grass and other useful or agreeable vegetable matter to the tune of $7,000,000 every year, and threaten to become rampant over the greater part of the entire country" (*L* 384). What Shepherd—and

by extension, Kingsolver—offer in place of this thoughtless racism is the humanistic reach of novel-writing. Through snippets of reviews on his first book
Vessels of Majesty, Kingsolver highlights how literary narrative can allow its
readers the critical capacity to look at history and the current political climate
with different eyes. Shepherd's novel enables one reader to *"understand the
Mexican Conquistadors through new eyes,"* (L 426) and pushes another to
consider *"how the boys on both sides of the war were still human whether the
Spanish or the Mexicans. Every person is human, even Japs, their mothers must
have all cried tears just the same* [italics in the original]" (L 427).

The effect of Shepherd's writing thereby speaks directly to Kingsolver's understanding that "art" must be aligned with "conscience" as manifested in "social criticism" (*HT* 229): writing is inevitably a political act, one that engages
with political rhetoric in order to realign our moral sensibilities. To reiterate
my argument, it is precisely the lacuna, as "crucial missing piece" (L 475), that
makes this reengagement possible: literature offers us imaginative variations of
what is possible, filling in the gap between historical determinism and utopian
potentiality. A big part of Shepherd's maturation as an artist is this realization
of the revolutionary impact of his art—the writer must embody a *different*
truth from that of the media. Kingsolver's figure for this is Communism.

Shepherd's Künstlerroman and Utopian Hope

Kingsolver's novel participates in the literary genre of the *Künstlerroman*,
which is a narrative about the maturation of an artist-figure. The young Shepherd is an avid reader, coping with his isolation and fear with books such as
"*The Mysterious Affair at Styles, The Count of Monte Cristo, Around the
World in Eighty Days* [and] *Twenty Thousand Leagues Under the Sea*" (L 22).
Shepherd's penchant for romance and adventure narratives color his experiences in Isla Pixol, where the natural surroundings are romanticized as part of
his quest for escape from his distant mother and a panoply of aloof and uncar-
ing adult figures. The lacuna which he spots whilst diving initially functions as
an otherworldly space wherein Shepherd's need for privacy finds a compelling
correlative. As he notices "a dark something, or really a dark nothing, a great
deep hole in the rock" (L 45), Shepherd claims this knowledge for his own,
eventually disappearing into the abyss of the fragmented narrative he has left
behind at the end of the novel.

Just as the young Stephen Dedalus in James Joyce's *A Portrait of the Artist as a Young Man* is initially influenced by his society's deep religiosity and
subservience to colonial authority before rejecting them entirely, the young
Shepherd's mind is suffused by images from colonial narratives of Spanish
conquest, uncritically imbibing the civilizing ethos that served to legitimize

European colonialization. Kingsolver returns to the brutal legacies of colonial rule, which she has explored in her earlier novel *The Poisonwood Bible*, detailing its influence on the ways we understand history, and the relationship between colonizer and colonized. As with *The Poisonwood Bible*, narrative form performs important work in the context of resisting this hegemonic version of history: by breaking up her narrative into fragments and multiple perspectives that demand active engagement in bringing together disparate viewpoints and timescales, Kingsolver's novels argue for a critical assessment of some of the foundational truths undergirding the experience of European modernity.

The crucial stage in Shepherd's development as an artist arrives when he is roped in to assist the Mexican painter, Diego Rivera. As Shepherd observes the unfolding of Rivera's mural on the walls of the National Palace, a new way of arranging, understanding, and interpreting history becomes evident:

> The people in the paintings are larger than the men in the offices. Dark brown women among jungle trees. Men cutting stone, weaving cloth, playing drums, carrying flowers as big as brooms. Quetzalcoatl sits at the center of one mural in his grand green-feathered headdress. Everyone is there: Indians with gold bracelets on brown arms, Porfirio Díaz with his tall white hair and French sword. In one corner sketch, a native *escuincle* dogs growls at the European sheep and cattle that have just arrived, as if he knows the trouble ahead. Cortés is there too, in the hallway outside Property Assessment. The Painter has made him look like a white-faced monkey in his crested helmet. Moctezuma kneels, while the Spaniards make their mischief: fat monks stealing bags of gold, the Indians enslaved. (L 89–90)

Rivera's mural is apposite to the overall aesthetic of Kingsolver's novel in that both utilize the jarring effects of fragmentation in the service of political critique. By allowing "everyone [to be] there" at once, the artwork powerfully suggests how the history of Mexico cannot be coopted into the hegemonic narrative of European modernity, of which colonialism and capitalist development play large roles in. The mural also employs the aesthetics of spatial form, which, as the scholar Joseph Frank has argued, forms a crucial component of modernist art. In the reception of spatial form, the viewer/reader is forced to make active connections between parts of the artwork that its creator has distributed throughout its uniqueness as aesthetic object. This spatiality once again challenges the ordinary conception of temporality as unbroken and singular, putting us in touch with multiple modes, or "centers," of interpretation.

As the mural indicates, no overarching "scene" of history is privileged; instead, the creative tensions and juxtapositions between self and other, modernity and premodernity are picked up and challenged. Lastly, Rivera's critique of colonialism is allied to his postmodernist presentation of history. The hallowed image that Shepherd has of Cortés is savagely undercut by Rivera's presentation of him as a "white-faced monkey," destabilizing the boundaries between (white) civility and animalism so as to expose the rapacity lying at the heart of the colonial enterprise. Kingsolver emphasizes here that it is the role of art to enlarge consciousness by making us face "uncomfortable truths" (*HT* 227). What is more, it has the capacity to change our very relationship with history and selfhood. Kingsolver highlights this by noting how Rivera's mural makes people uncomfortable: "some people want him torn down, not just gringos but also the Mexican boys in *tejano* hats who don't want anyone saying that they were born from between the legs of an Indian woman" (*L* 171). Shepherd's ultimate integrity to his art is also born from his unshakeable belief that it voices truths to power by challenging powerful ideologies and accultured ways of understanding the world.

For Kingsolver art's truth provides an ethical corrective against propaganda and jingoism because it cannot be integrated with the status quo. The novel's bitter antipathy against media sensationalism stems from Kingsolver's own personal "Trial by Headline" (Sheehan 206), which she faced after 9/11, aligning her own recalcitrance with that of Shepherd's. *The Lacuna* alludes to the Bonus Army demonstrations of 1932 to indict media outlets for betraying the demands of the protestors, while justifying police brutality against them. As Shepherd points out, the demonstrators are presented via the "news headline" (*L* 130) as subversive malcontents who are unpatriotic. The media's ability to sway public opinion against the disenfranchised speaks to the dangerous commodification of information and truth to suit prepackaged ideology. As Kingsolver observes, "to buy and sell information as nothing more than a consumer product, like soda pop, is surely wrong. Marketed in that way, information's principal attribute must be universal palpability" (*HT* 226). In the context of the novel, this sentiment is manifested in Douglas McArthur's "opinion [that] the Bonus Army consists of Communists and persons with criminal records" (*L* 143), a convenient way to rally support behind the military's actions based on a classification of the discontents as threatening to the heteronormative way of life.

Kingsolver's disdain of the mass media resonates with some of the sociological theories articulated by the Frankfurt School of critical theory. For these theorists heteronormative culture, as shaped by mass conformity to the social arrangements necessitated by capitalism, traps individuals in ideological unfreedom toward the diminished conditions of their existences. The culture industry already programs reactions based on the uniformity of its products; critical thinking as reflection about the falsity of these conditions is repressed and forbidden. Kingsolver's contextualization of the far-reaching nature of this is seen in her charting of America's response to the Bonus Army dissidents, suspected Communists under the McCarthy years, and the contemporary "war on terror" post 9/11: there is a consistent pattern of "wanting to believe in heroes . . . and villains . . . when [the polity is] very frightened [as] it's less taxing than the truth" (*L* 321). In contrast Shepherd and Kingsolver offer their readers art that gives voice to "oppression" (*L* 374) and suffering by standing at a distance from easy moral absolutes. The desire of the genuine artist "to tell the truth" (*L* 261) must be articulated at variance from the simplifications of political rhetoric. As the philosophers Theodor Adorno and Max Horkheimer write, "the moment in which the work of art by which it transcends reality cannot, indeed, be severed from style; that moment, however, does not consist in achieved harmony, in the questionable unity of form and content, inner and outer, individual and society, but in those traits in which the discrepancy emerges, in the necessary failure of the passionate striving for identity" (103). By pursuing an aesthetic of fragmentation, wherein readerly attention is drawn toward breaks and gaps, Kingsolver sees style as political commentary: the work of art cannot unite itself with any single political ideology, but must suggest the indirect, fragmented approach to truth. Shepherd's own entanglements with Communism demonstrate his paradoxical commitment to intransigence and fidelity toward "what-might-have-been."

Communism, Utopian Potential, Hope, and Difference

Kingsolver's engagement with the fraught topic of Communism as political ideology informs Shepherd's final existential assertion of his integrity as a writer. As an alternative system of political economy, Communism provides Kingsolver with one more avenue to pursue the notion of difference. Apart from any discussion of its feasibility, Kingsolver latches on to the conceptual alterity of Communism to hint at its revolutionary potential. This potential carries within it the seeds of utopia inasmuch as it suggests ways in which society could be constructed differently from what it is now. The Russian Revolution is therefore significant as it purports to "send the monarchs packing, along with all the rich bloodsuckers living off the workers and the peasants" (*L* 190). For Shepherd, Leo Trotsky emerges as a figure whose zeal and passion for his cause present an opportunity for history to be reimagined; he is appropriately characterized by Shepherd as a world-historical personage who is "hard enough to bend [history's] edge" (*L* 478). However, Kingsolver tempers this idealism with a melancholic awareness that the historical imagination is as much conditioned by the promise of revolution as with revolution's eventual defeat. Shepherd's recognition of the transience of historical circumstance emerges in his commentary that "the great Spanish empire has collapsed into one small landmass of rock and vineyard, the little right paw of Europe" (*L* 536), with this statement providing an ironic reflection on the eventual collapse of similar political projects. Trotsky is defeated both by the superior cunning of Stalin and the tarnishing of his name in the newspapers: the media "from France and the United States [call] him a villain, and the Mexican ones [label] him a 'villain in our midst'" (*L* 203). Indeed, it is the traumatic impact of Trotsky's brutal murder that sends Shepherd into exile and seclusion—he relocates from Mexico City to Asheville, North Carolina, carrying within him an utter disillusionment about the failed prospects of the revolution that Trotsky symbolizes.

However, we may argue here that the presence of Trotsky *haunts* Shepherd, in that he is called to respond and to make peace with the missed opportunity of Communist revolution through his writing. In this way, Communism emerges as a radically unfinished project that, for Kingsolver, carries with it a utopian promise of difference. Inasmuch as Communism projects a radical insistence that reality and history must be conceived on an alternative basis, it remains as a powerful tool of critique. This promise (which must always remain unfulfilled) is described by the philosopher Jacques Derrida as such: "the effectivity or actuality of . . . the communist promise will always keep within it, and it must do so, this absolutely undetermined messianic hope at its heart, this eschatological relation of the to-come of an event *and* of a singularity, of an alterity that cannot be anticipated" (81). This hope, pledged to the future, resonates with the novel's controlling image of the lacuna so as to insist on an absence that can dislocate (and relocate) the sense of who we are as contemporary political and historical beings: "A blank space on a form, a missing page, a void, a hole in your knowledge of someone—it's still some real *thing*" (*L* 464).

In this way Kingsolver continually emphasizes that the lacuna is paradoxically the most important thing about a story, for the breaks come to stand for the chance for change. The final sections of the novel depict a hearing where Shepherd stands before the HUAC to face charges of communist activity. Presented as a dialogue, this section casts Shepherd as a Socratic-type figure who is similarly accused of crimes pertaining to the corruption of the citizens of the state. More indirectly, Shepherd incarnates the spectral presence of Trotsky through his being decried and persecuted as a Communist. Shepherd's fate thereby emphasizes how he is "a person called to pursue his own difference over the human patterns possible" (Wagner-Martin, *Barbara Kingsolver's World* 184), this difference allowing him to create art that taps upon the wellsprings of unrealized potential: "You asked me why I've stayed here so long. I can try to say. People have a lot of color and songs in Mexico, more art than they have hopes, it often seemed to me. Here, I found people bursting with hope but not many songs. They didn't sing, they turned on the radio. They wanted stories, like anything. So I decided to try my hand at making art for the hopeful. Because I wasn't good at the other thing, manufacturing hopes for the artful" (*L* 646).

Shepherd's ultimate disappearance after the trial (seemingly a suicide-by-drowning) represents an utter refusal to be reabsorbed into the structures of meaning that have marginalized his individuality. His fate remains a mystery, and his wisdom is forever meant to be understood asymptotically from the mainstream. However, Kingsolver ends the novel with an important emphasis on the preservation of his history by Violet. As much as history is a narrative fraught with contradictions, inconsistencies, and systemic biases, it is also that which enables us to seek connection between present circumstances and past crises. Kingsolver thus legitimizes the need for history to be recorded and archived so as to preserve an intelligible directionality in the face of transience and erosion. It is as much a mistake to impose a monolithic perspective on historical events as it is "that a man should disappear" (*L* 348) because the archival evidence is constantly threatened by oblivion. It is Violet, the female writer and archivist, who has the final say by entrusting the final shape of the novel to posterity: "I dread to do what I do now, commending a man's life into the bleak passage to some other place, be it filled with light and darkness" (*L* 670). This (re)construction of the past as hermeneutic propaedeutic toward charting a future is taken up in her next novel *Unsheltered*, placing at the forefront the anonymous yet momentous labor generations of women carry out to build and preserve new worlds.

The Presentation of Crisis in *Unsheltered* as Enabling an Intellectual Legacy

Kingsolver reengages the political crisis of America in terms of a battle between "the investigators and the sweeteners" (*U* 41): the world is divided into people who observe reality closely and thereby change it, and those who stubbornly cling onto the privileges afforded to them as part of the status quo, even though the foundations upon which those privileges are constructed are surely crumbling away. *Unsheltered* is Kingsolver's attempt to understand what American citizenry and political ideals have become under the leadership of Donald Trump; as Ron Charles notes in a review of the novel, "here comes the first major novel to tackle the Trump era straight on and place in it the larger chronicle of existential threats" (1). Although never explicitly mentioned by name, Trump's presence is recorded in the novel through the protagonist Willa

Knox's description of him as a "tyrant" and a "granny, self-aggrandizing man" (*U* 352) whose campaigning aims to "bring back yesterday" (*U* 249). As Kingsolver notes with ironic despair, Trump's appeal is historical to the extent that his opportunism feeds into white insecurity that the "traditional" values upon which America has been built are coming under assault, a false racial ideology based on fear of the other that *The Lacuna* has already criticized.

Kingsolver locates the characters in the novel within two distinct time periods, with their narratives being linked by the fact that they reside in Vineland, New Jersey: the contemporary period is focalized around Willa, an ex-journalist who has quit her job so as to accompany her Greek husband Iano, a struggling academic forced to relocate after his previous college shut down, and the older timeframe concerns itself with a schoolteacher, Thatcher Greenwood, who bonds with his eccentric neighbor Mary Treat, while facing professional discrimination because he is determined to teach the fledging principles of Darwinian evolution in the face of religious conservatism. What links Kingsolver's toggling between these two periods are thematic resonances across chronology associated with charting the way forward in uncertain times. Indeed, Kingsolver begins the novel with a notice given to Willa that her "foundation is nonexistent" (*U* 1): the house which her family is currently residing in rests on shaky grounds and will collapse. Kingsolver employs this architectural metaphor to extend from Willa's own family situation to an entire nation desperate to cling "to a century-old vision of America" (*U* 99) at the cost of buying into racist propaganda and unenlightened social policies. As Willa's narrative lays out, her family is threatened with economic uncertainty and fear for the future: Iano has "taken [up] a teaching position that was an insult to someone with his credentials," (*U* 12) and Willa is suddenly saddled with her son Zeke's baby after his wife unexpectedly commits suicide due to postpartum depression. Kingsolver convincingly charts Willa's despair at the shape of her life, with her despairing at how "two hardworking people [could] do everything right in life and arrive at their fifties essentially destitute" (*U* 11).

For Kingsolver this awareness of destitution and bankruptcy modulates into an existential weariness that capitalist consumption and environmental destruction have brought humanity to a tipping point that cannot be reversed. This point is made via a heated conversation between Zeke and his sister Antigone during a family dinner. As ideological positions on the need for capitalist growth versus reversing economic inequality are debated, Kingsolver rehearses the dilemmas of our contemporary political situation, implying that there is no one single panacea that can resolve the contradictions between consumption and conservation:

> "Keep telling yourself that. Helping rich people get richer is socially responsible."
>
> "Look, money's engine and it's out there running day and night, whether you like it or not. For bad or for good. The global move to divest South Africa is what finally brought down the apartheid regime. You can't dispute that."
>
> […]
>
> Tig rolled her eyes. "Humans have outgrown the carrying capacity of the planet. The responsible thing would be to *shrink* our bottom line."
>
> "Hey, gee, we tried that! For five centuries before the Industrial Revolution. It was called the Dark Ages." (*U* 65)

In a novel "brimming with big ideas and long conversations" (Nilanjana 1), Kingsolver presents the contemporary moment as in need of urgent redefinition. The image of collapse and catastrophe implies that preserving outworn and outdated ideas about society can only lead to stultification and ethical impasse. As Kingsolver analyzes it, human beings are a product of their own existential situations inasmuch as their opinions and actions reflect the dominant ideologies of their present times: "Zeke embodied the contradiction of his generation: jaded about the fate of the world, idealistic about personal prospects. A house built on easy courage. And Tig in her way was also brave, dissecting the world as she saw it, believing her strategies mattered" (*U* 68). It is in the debate between old, established ideas and newer ones that Kingsolver believes change and redefinition is possible; as with her other novels, Kingsolver rejects monological and totalistic ways of viewing the world and historical circumstances in favor of dialogue, conversation, and embracing multiplicity.

In the political context of the novel, this exchange functions as a powerful argument for diversity, and a strong rejection of ultra-conservative attitudes that have distressingly surfaced in real-world political discourse. The presentation of crisis, although not explicitly focalized through environmental issues, allows Kingsolver to raise similar questions in this novel as she does in *Flight Behavior*: How does impending catastrophe offer humanity a chance to redefine the ways in which we live our lives, and to envision alternative possibilities of existence and sociality? In this way Kingsolver's metaphorical image of the architectural structure of the domicile that is constantly under threat of collapse unites her two historical epochs that see themselves on the verge of transition toward something new and undefined. As the debate carries on between preserving the old ways of the world and the need for reconstruction, Kingsolver employs the historical perspective afforded by fiction to dramatize the agonistic struggle between maintaining the status quo and the confronting of difference as challenge to received wisdom: "I understand the appeal of retaining an old structure rather than paying to tear it down before rebuilding. . . . We are often persuaded that what is convenient is also right. But these associates were not architects. Their idea was unsound" (*U* 130).

Kingsolver's reference to "architecture," or conceptual design, is developed at great length in terms of the battle between evolutionism and creationism, ideas that set the context for the narrative involving Thatcher and Mary. Thatcher's initial acquaintance with his eccentric neighbor who is more attached to plants and insects than with people develops into a lifelong admiration of how she stands for observation and reason in the face of unreflective dogmatic assumptions about the world. Mary's example allows Thatcher to revise his Victorian attitudes toward the value of a woman's work—he sees that he has mistaken Mary's devotion to science as "an abandoned wife's loneliness" (*U* 86). Mary's passionate exposition of the principles of natural selection positions "men like Darwin and Gray [as] earnest investigators at the frontier of a new world" (*U* 268); they advance knowledge about human history and possibility at the expense of what Mary disdains as old mythologies. Kingsolver's own views are clearly reflected in Mary's: as she writes in her essay "A Fist in the Eye of God," Darwin's theory of natural selection and modification is, in the eyes of contemporary biology, "the greatest, simplest, most elegant logical construct ever to dawn across our curiosity about the workings of natural life" and "the most robust unifying explanation ever devised in biological science" (*SW* 96). This encomium for Darwin is heightened in *Unsheltered* through Kingsolver's emphasis on the potentially revolutionary nature of its explanatory framework. By dislodging the age-old idea that human beings are afforded primacy within nature as beings created in God's image, evolution rejects the notion that "life can only be worth having if the deliberate business of life belongs to [mankind] only" (*U* 87). Kingsolver's aim in shifting the timeframe of her narrative back to the middle of the nineteenth century is not only to present the afterlife of once-revolutionary intellectual ideas, but also to dramatize the iconoclastic aspect of these ideas as they come to unseat traditional concepts concerning ecology, religion, and science. Mary thus notes that "men . . . dread new views, for fear they'll have to set aside their hard-earned credentials and begin their climb again at the bottom rung" (*U* 268)—the clinging onto old ideas is as much motivated by gender politics as it is by intellectual conservatism.

What Kingsolver's resuscitation of this age-old debate through historical fiction reveals is the (as-yet) unrealized ethical potentialities behind evolution. Understanding evolution not only trains us in the virtues of "good science"

(*SW* 96) by emphasizing the Enlightenment virtues of reason and positivism instead of putting our faith in "the insecurities of certain ideologues" (*SW* 96), but also stresses our biological commonalities with nonhuman forms of life— we are all bound by the same pressures of survival as adapting to the changing conditions of our environment. As Mary opines, her observation on the ways her plant species modify themselves to adapt makes her feel "as if [humans and plants] are of the same world" (*U* 83). Kingsolver's ecocritical thought appropriately meshes with her political commentary: if we, like the spiders that adroitly construct their homes, are bound by the same "want for shelter" (*U* 88), then negotiating ethical and political possibilities in a world that is crumbling under the weight of environmental degradation requires a holistic redesign, a rebuilding that becomes necessary to advance society. The atavism that Trump represents is, for Kingsolver, a dangerous retreat into questionable beliefs about American exceptionalism and white privilege.

Thatcher and Mary's story is then as much about holding on to the values of scientific inquiry in the face of persecution as it is about seeking out truth. For Mary, "truth is not ours to find within, but to search without" (*U* 151): the concept does not depend on supernatural revelation, but instead on self-determination. The various public debates pitting Thatcher against members of his community who decry evolution as an assault on Christianity demonstrate how the authentic notion of truth necessarily proves to be upsetting to the status quo. In place of the picture of "the universe [as] a mystery sprung from God's mind" (*U* 321), Thatcher offers an understanding of reality that "uses nothing outside the evidence to make our explanations" (*U* 335). The arguments about the "architecture" of the universe pit simplicity and elegance against incomprehensibility, an attempt that "will always grow more complex as it [aims] to patch its own holes" (*U* 336). The demagogues who oppose Thatcher in these debates consistently manage to drum up crowd support to silence him. This haranguing demonstrates how the same mechanisms of censorship and repression work in twentieth century America as they did in the same country a century earlier (as presented in *The Lacuna*): the seditious Darwinists are characterized as "atheists" (*U* 333) who must be guarded against.

In this way Kingsolver validates her practice of historical fiction insofar as it allows us to place certain human tendencies within a wider perspective. As Kingsolver sees it, people will always tend to gravitate toward maintaining the status quo as a reaction against the revolutionary import of fresh ideas. The negative response against the truth that Thatcher advocates for helps explain how the magnetism of a Trump becomes possible; as Mary notes, "when men fear the loss of what they know, they will follow any tyrant who promises to restore the old order" (*U* 206). Kingsolver's presentation of the largely forgotten Mary Treat is not only a tribute to the anonymous intellectuals who push history forward, but also a celebration of feminist self-determination. As Braidotti notes, "feminists were raised on rational argumentation and detached self-irony" ("In spite of the times" 3), traits which Mary consistently embodies. Indeed, if "feminism is regarded as a 'child' of the Enlightenment, and the Enlightenment is positioned as inherently secular or anti-religion" (Browne 768), then one of Kingsolver's aims is to foreground feminist work in the development of modern ideas on selfhood and society. This "rescuing" of Mary's story is as much the writer's mission as it is the archivist who reactivates the past by carrying on the work of history.

The need to preserve the past lest it falls into oblivion not only motivates Willa to investigate the circumstances surrounding Mary and Thatcher, but also provides a measure of clarity about her existential deadlock. Desperate to hold on to the family house, Willa decides to check whether it qualifies for a state heritage grant due to its having housed these two historical personae. What initially begins as a practical inquiry into the possibilities of receiving financial benefit to preserve and renovate the house turns into a more sustained quest for enlightenment about the work that previous generations have done in order to pave the way for the future. As she utilizes her aptitude for research, honed in her previous occupation as a reporter, Willa becomes an informal archivist whose work resembles Violet Brown in that both practice a feminine mode of recording, analyzing, and integrating data within a complex, multilayered historical narrative.

For Willa, "the mélange of personal artifacts [which she uncovers in the course of her research on Vineland] no longer oppressed but consoled her, proof of many eccentric individualities surviving against the long odds of being erased by time" (*U* 228): the historical record is *queered* to the extent that research uncovers multiple little narratives that enrich existential possibilities in the present. To reiterate Colebrook's argument at the start of this chapter, we become historical beings insofar as our relationship to history and the archive is incomplete. Kingsolver brings a feminist inflection to this theoretical claim in positioning Willa and Mary as continuing a conversation across time, demonstrating how breaking free of the stranglehold of capitalist consumption and environmental exploitation can be possible if "humans could view the world with less immediate self-interest" (*SW* 65).

For Willa, the ethical injunction that Mary's attitude toward scientific inquiry surfaces is evident in how she is "seemingly able to forget human cravings and immerse herself in the nonhuman lives around her" (*U* 228)—a shift away from anthropocentric ways of thought toward attending to the world incarnates an ecocritical stance which opens up a more positive relationship with regards to otherness. Kingsolver thereby demonstrates how the work of ecofeminism is always necessarily incomplete in that it ceaselessly works to provide a conceptual alternative toward heteronormative practices as they manifest across historical epochs. The task of critique is renewed in the lives of women whose eccentric visions harness the potentialities of difference to effect political change and intervention. A feminist mode of historiography thus deeply unsettles the quotidian understanding of time as linear passage from the past toward the future—the gaps and absences within the historical record must be reenergized, not toward restoring the contentious image of the past, but to seize historical crisis *as* crisis so as to (re)activate the unanswered questions history poses for us. Kingsolver thereby agrees with Giovanni Zapperi's observation of feminist archival research "not as a nostalgic operation, but rather as a powerful form of reactivation" (45).

It seems as if repetition and readjustment are important modes for historical consciousness; as the philosopher Gilles Deleuze argues, repetition is genuine if it brings into being something completely new in each of its iterations. Time is therefore not regarded as an indifferent succession of monadic moments that have no relationship with one another; instead, each moment is suffused with a potentiality-to-be which alters an entire understanding of temporality *from within* itself. Kingsolver demonstrates the linkages between the past and present by having her chapters "flow" into one another: while the narrative alternates between the past and present, the concluding words of the previous chapter are repeated in the title of the next one. Philosophical concepts are repeated across time periods, with the later repetition of the concept not only hearkening back to its prior use, but also allowing the reader to reactivate his or her understanding of it in the context of the present. Thatcher's explanation of Occam's Razor in the context of the theory of natural selection positions evolution as a superior theory because "the less adorned explanation is the one more directly tested, and more plainly proven" (*U* 336). This logic is reactivated in the present-day conversation between Antigone and her borderline racist grandfather Nick who believes climate change to be a "shit hoax" (*U* 368). As Antigone vehemently explains, "when there's a lot of different explanations for something . . . including supernatural and voodoo, you have to go with the simplest one. You look at *just* the evidence, nothing extra thrown in, and then go with simple" (*U* 369). Indeed, Antigone's teacherly manner as she says these words aptly mirror Thatcher's devotion to "teach truth instead of mythology" (*U* 125), arguing for the continuing need of education to demystify and provide clarity into our contemporary situation. The constant battle between uncomfortable truths and convenient ideologies allows Kingsolver to seek congruences between the contemporary issue of climate change denial,

Thatcher's getting into trouble with his school authorities for teaching evolution, and the real-life "Scopes trial" (*U* 287) whose effects are still being felt in American schools.

For Kingsolver, fiction can imbue historical events and turning points with affective immediacy; we feel the contemporary impact of these intellectual ideas as they shift, upset, and ultimately challenge the structures through which we comprehend our humanity and place in the world. Crucially Kingsolver's employment of historical fiction is decidedly anti-postmodern insofar as it abstains from questioning the veracity of historical reality or to suggest the ultimate unattainability of truth; I argue instead for an interpretive imbrication of fiction and reality which retrieves the "muteness" of the historical record so as to allow narrative to confer significance to historical circumstances. In other words, history becomes a hermeneutic resource that enlarges possibilities for action and responsibility in the real world—we *un*cover to *re*cover and *dis*cover.

Kingsolver's novel is thus ultimately about survival and continuation as *adaptation* to new conditions of thought and ways of living. To recover an unmediated representation of Mary from an overarching historical perspective that has traditionally marginalized and silenced women is impossible, for the record has privileged the achievements of men such as Darwin as the father of modern biology. To return to Willa, her intrepid archival work is important so that the story of Mary can be told; without her, Mary "falls through the cracks" as her epistolary correspondence with Darwin would be categorized as "personal" (*U* 285) and not professional. Once again, the image of cracks and rents within the record provides a compelling metaphor through which to describe the ways in which history can be retold from the margins. If women are "othered" from the official narrative of Western cultural history, their stories must come to fill in the lacuna that splinters this account of history, not in order to supplement patriarchal norms, but to suggest a powerful revolutionary bent that fractures this account more. As Elizabeth Clark writes, the woman "leaves her traces, through whose exploration, as they are embedded in a larger social-linguistic framework, she lives on" (31). What Mary comes to represent for Willa, as she does for Kingsolver and her readers, is the inauguration of the entirely new, the promise of rebuilding society for the better as it crumbles around us: "Willa was riveted [by Mary], ahead of [her] time. . . . Mary's correspondence with her scientist friends suggested the gentle Victorians of Vineland, and America for that matter, had shit for brains. . . . A great shift was dawning, with the human masters' place in the kingdom much reduced from its former glory. She could see how this might lead to a sense of complete disorientation in the universe" (*U* 391).

It is by filling in the gaps with reference to Mary's narrative that Willa is able to sublimate her anxieties and worries about the uncharted and unsheltered future by contextualizing how history is written from out of crisis. Mary's example inspires Willa by showing her how courage and dedication to a cause allow her to "move . . . beyond herself" (*U* 406). The novel concludes with a coming-into-birth of Willa the historian who devotes herself to reviving the lost correspondence between Mary and Thatcher; as she senses it, this labor of love will be as much archival as it is creative, transforming our contemporary understanding of Mary and retrieving new possibilities for feminist self-determination in a world growing increasingly benighted and shut off from change: "A Greenwood-Treat correspondence existed somewhere, she knew this in her bones, and she would be the one to find it. Taking custody of other lives felt as large in its demands as birthing a child. Holding other eyes inside her line of sight, other futures and risks, would mean making something new—even if new was impossible because they were all made of just one set of molecules" (*U* 452). In a word adaptation is both possible and necessary in order to fashion new shelters from unfinished historical projects. What is more, "history is shaped . . . by what people, theories, buildings and legacies survive" (Hazelton 1); this not only bequeaths a sense of continuation and heritage to our present endeavors, but also presents the future as opportunity to readjust our concepts and ideas in the service of fashioning better ones. Kingsolver's utopian vision is as much embedded in her landscapes as it is in this approach to history and the making of it.

Kingsolver's recent turn toward historical fiction thus cannot be separated from her abiding concern with the power of difference that comes to unsettle and trouble the hegemonic imposition of heteronormative concepts from within, a theme that (as I have argued in this book) unifies her work from *The Bean Trees* onward. The ability to encounter difference as uncanny alternative, and not as inferior substitute or repetition of the same, is crucial to enabling a reevaluation of many, if not all, of the fundamental tenets of capitalist modernity. To seek a consistent ethical vision in Kingsolver that informs her multivarious presentations of locales and situations from Africa to the American South is to understand her work in terms of a constant negotiation of the spaces in between cultures, ethnicities, genders, and histories. These liminal narratives, or narratives of liminalities, open up consideration of what society *can be* when its members break down conceptual barriers that reinforce outworn distinctions separating self from other, art from politics, and culture from environment. For Kingsolver, history is both a mournful record of mankind's inherent tendencies toward groupthink, unenlightened conformity, and rejection of new ways of thinking, and a chance to approach these injustices with more emancipatory lenses and sensibilities. Her grounding of a utopian politics within the everyday—as demonstrated through sustainable agricultural and food practices, restorative justice for minorities, and widening notions of "natural" community that recognize birthright and societal nurturance—is not another species of wishful thinking and "ivory tower" whimsicality; instead, it is reimagining utopia as *other*worldly, or a world that can be *other to itself*, carrying within it the seeds of hope that life can be lived along different guidelines and emphases.

Throughout this book I have read Kingsolver as a gentle, loving critic of ecology, one whose concerns are not limited to any particular social or political sphere. Rather, Kingsolver's ethical intervention targets an entire ecology of thinking and practice, aiming to readjust our fundamental (self-)images of family, history, and finally, world. These layers variously intersect and diverge, allowing for literary art to stress interrelation and concatenation in ways that break down boundaries between the private and the public, the personal and the social. Kingsolver's politics is in the last word a politics starting and ending at the level of the everyday, for it is from there that change is grounded in the achievable and possible. To end this chapter by quoting from the American poet Wallace Stevens (who Kingsolver uses as the epigraph to *Unsheltered*), fiction is an image of the world wherein we "find [ourselves] more truly and more strange" (53), unhoused but defiantly free to carry on retooling it.

CHAPTER 6

Debilitating Consumption
and the Will to Survive
Demon Copperhead

Kingsolver's newest novel *Demon Copperhead* represents an intriguing modulation of many of the persistent themes this book has followed. Her first novel to sustain an intertextual link with an established classic of Victorian fiction (and to adopt a fully masculine narratorial perspective), *Demon Copperhead* transposes Dickens's narrative of growth and self-knowledge in the context of her protagonist's desperate struggles to find his purpose amidst a social backdrop of poverty, neglect, and debilitating addiction. In an almost nightmarish evocation of the dysfunctional social systems that crush the potentialities of children by dooming them to a life of dependency and violence, Kingsolver updates Dickens's diagnoses of the political and social ills that cramp and suffocate the vulnerable as part of the human cost of a rapidly modernizing England. Kingsolver explicitly acknowledges her artistic debt to Dickens for *David Copperfield*, lauding him for "his impassioned critique of institutional poverty and its damaging effects on children in his society" (*DC* 547). Her admiration of the Victorian novelist's ability to use his writing to shed an important spotlight on social issues clearly channels her own purposes in harnessing her craft toward challenging deeply held beliefs about class and adolescence.

As this chapter will analyze, the narrative *telos* of the *Bildungsroman* is as central to Kingsolver as it was for Dickens. Both writers use the form to explore the questions involving integration, vocational purpose, and the adoption of a mature perspective through which to allow the larger "shape" of society to emerge and become a theme for artistic exploration. The forward movement of the narrative constantly pits personal expectation against societal resistance, framing the widening growth of individual aspiration within the societal limitations imposed by others in order to examine engagement as possibility, personal emergence as tenuous accomplishment. Writing about the nineteenth-century *Bildungsroman*, Frederic Jameson argues that the technique functions as "an instrument for the exploration of the new possibilities of bourgeois society, a kind of registering device, the establishment of a laboratory situation in which those possibilities can be acted out before our eyes" (281). I echo Jameson's assessment of the value of possibility in the context of Kingsolver's employment of her protagonist as a conduit for registering the negative impact of capitalism as it transforms and deforms ways of being, knowing, and sharing resources. Happily these factors ultimately do not impinge on the moral worth of the protagonist and his final ability to rise above circumstances and to achieve a tentative reckoning with a past he has both introjected and transcended. Even in this most recent novel of hers, the impetuses of ecocritical thought can still be traced, for just as care for the environment is made more difficult by the constraints of rural poverty in *Flight Behavior*, this novel demonstrates how ethical choices that bring about self-awareness are limited by economic deprivation. Ecocriticism is thus a framework that identifies and criticizes world systems of inequity and dominance fueling the unsustainable continuation of the Anthropocene—*Demon Copperhead* forms an important part of Kingsolver's ongoing writerly resistance to the "logic" of the normal.

I will first explore the thematic connections between *Demon Copperhead* and *David Copperfield*. Unpacking the similarities and divergences between these two novels will allow us to understand some of the motivations behind Kingsolver's updating of Dickens's narrative in the context of the contemporary opioid crisis in America, which she diagnoses as one of the most pressing public health catastrophes in recent years. Kingsolver's interest in charting the progression of her protagonist Demon from his birth to his emergence as a successful comic strip artist once again registers her investment in the symbiotic relationship between her characters and their environment. Insofar as Demon recognizes that a "kid born to a junkie is a junkie. He'll grow up to be everything you don't want to know" (*DC* 2), he highlights how addiction becomes a potent symbol of how systems of neglect and exploitation entrap individuals within a parasitic economy of use and abuse they cannot escape from. What this implies is that Kingsolver understands addiction to be a symptom of capitalism's insidious reach over our collective bodies: the disenfranchised members of Lee County are afforded little options to think outside of "poverty [and] short life expectance" (*DC* 416) that seem to be their gloomy inheritance as a result of inegalitarian economic practices. In other words if Dickens was himself interested in how human beings are chained to "an unknowable past, a haunted present, [and] a mortgaged future" (Dever 216), this inevitability structures Demon's quest throughout the novel to find and forge a place for himself that "is not going to swallow [him] alive" (*DC* 3).

My subsequent analysis of the novel spotlights Kingsolver's controlling metaphor of consumption, which not only details the characters' struggles with addiction as debilitating force and desire ("a craving [that] can ratchet itself up and up inside a body and mind, at the same time that body's strength for tolerating its favorite drug goes down and down" [*DC* 109]), but also alludes to how individuals are maimed and destroyed by economic and political systems that prioritize consumption and expenditure over care and nurturance. In this way Kingsolver revisits her major novelistic themes concerning political and ecological justice in a narrative that, on first read, is her bleakest and most jagged presentation of a society that constantly disappoints those it should be taking care of. As Annette Federico writes apropos *David Copperfield*, "Dickens recognized that there was much collective work to be done in the project of achieving social and economic justice. But he also famously saw the psychic damage caused by economic and educational systems that pretend to find arithmetical solutions to the problem of human unhappiness" (70–71). Reading *Demon Copperhead* in the light of its precursor reveals how the opportunities for genuine happiness are precious, fragile, and more often than not, deceptive and illusory. Kingsolver's novel is thereby balanced between a recognition that the body is vulnerable to its cravings, that it "can put you on detention away from all pleasures, but still make you write out the list of its needs" (*DC* 505), and an inchoate desire for a vocation that allows for autonomy and clarified vision through which healing from past traumas become articulable possibilities.

Reading Demon Copperhead with David Copperfield

Dickens's and Kingsolver's novels demonstrate a movement into self-determination that does not arrive without an attendant loss of innocence. Classic readings of *David Copperfield* as an example of the Victorian *Bildungsroman* emphasize how the concern with maturation and growth of its protagonist betokens an attendant loss of innocence that can only be imperfectly recaptured through reminiscence and the reconstructive power of narrative. As Bert Hornback writes about Dickens's novel, "David is required to relinquish his innocence, and the world which he meets beyond this innocence contains all the evil which the novel describes" (78). David has to endure the neglect and overt abuse administered by his stepfather Murdstone, suffer the loss of his mother and infant brother, and be painfully disabused of his former inaccurate assessments of childhood friendship with Steerforth and marital bliss with Dora

Spenlow as part of his journey. Part of Dickens's melancholic rendering of David's attainment of final "domestic joy" (866) with Agnes is his recognition of the diminishing of individual expectations that arrive with the magnitude of his losses throughout the course of the novel. For Alan Barr, David confronts the loss of innocence "repeatedly" (63), deflecting but not completely evading the implications of this disappearance as he reconstructs his narrative. The middle-class domesticity David settles into at the end of the novel, which seeks to reaffirm Victorian values, inadvertently reveals "an uneasy, compromised reality" (Barr 77). As other critics have noted, David cannot hide "a tone of regret and self-suppression" (Federico 91) as he acknowledges the lingering effects his memories have on his present self-understanding. Kingsolver's novel intensifies this sense of loss, betrayal, and disappointment by immersing the reader in the painful realities associated with addiction and coping with addiction in ways that combine the fairy-tale elements of Dickens's novel with the tough grittiness of contemporary novelists such as Irvine Welsh or Douglas Stuart.

As Demon is moved from foster home to foster home, he encounters situation after situation of exploitation that confirms him as disempowered and vulnerable, with no recourse to change his circumstances for the better. Kingsolver's almost vitriolic presentation of poverty affecting an entire community realigns the Victorian ideals of bourgeois self-sufficiency that Dickens promotes as desired end point for David's narrative; if the "qualities of self-reliant, Protestant, modern rational fortitude" (Buzard 236) are what enables David to transcend his straightened circumstances and achieve fame and security as a writer, these values alone are less likely to allow somebody from Demon's background to overcome his or her crippling disadvantages. As Demon states, "mountain people, country and farm people, we are nowhere the hell. It's a situation, being invisible. You can get to a point of needing to make the loudest possible noise just to see if you are still alive" (*DC* 377). Far from the Victorian *Bildungsroman* affirming what Franco Moretti calls a conversative "culture of stability and conformity" (181) to be found in the reconciliation between individual striving and social purpose, Kingsolver narrates Demon's growth *against* the backdrop of dysfunction and crisis, arguing for a mature perspective that provides him with "the tools to criticize [his] society and the social processes" (Kuehn 34) that have molded him to be who he is. Revisiting the theme of creative difference that I have pursued throughout his book as crucial to Kingsolver's aesthetic vision, Demon's maturity enables him to break free from the destructive cycle and logic that has claimed the lives of the many in his community: "I was past sorry for myself. Like every boy in Lee County I was raised to be a proud mule in a world that has scant use for mules. I'd tried the popular solutions to that problem, which generally pointed to early death. *The trick was to find others*" (DC 531, emphasis added).

To put the same point differently, Kingsolver's employment of the *Bildungsroman* suggests that the model of the self as (re)constructed by narrative cannot be a straightforward endorsement of the values of society, for the point is surely to search for self-understanding at a distance from preestablished ideas about an individual's place and potentiality within that society. Much of *Demon Copperhead* concerns itself with Demon's struggles to find existential purpose and direction within a society that affords little opportunity to realize human potential and capability, and it is Kingsolver's ethical aim to suggest that such realization outside of the domination of the economic logic of exploitation is possible. Demon's maturation is thereby a process of self-recognition, wherein the achievement of selfhood at the end of the novel signals an "ability to re-create his younger self with his feelings and responses, and at the same time to judge him" (Simon 45). The balance between empathy and critical distance emerges more strongly in Kingsolver than in Dickens—in contrast to *David Copperfield*'s tendency to draw a clear line between "good" and "bad" characters, *Demon Copperhead* implies how characters become products of their environments. While Dickens suggests a fundamental incompatibility between David and his "child-wife" Dora, Kingsolver depicts Demon's recognition of his culpability in enabling Dori's substance addiction and subsequent death from lethal overdose. In this way Demon's narrative once again evinces Kingsolver's interest in characters who work through their traumas in ways that can help them articulate new possibilities of being.

As it emerges by the end of the novel, Demon is still in the process of reconciling the fact that he has survived and conquered his addiction with the many who have succumbed to the pattern of existence that seems to be his community's damaged destiny: "My predecessor Collins. Cush Polk, a cruelty to make you tear your hair. He had OD'd on what must have been his very first step off the narrow path" (DC 539). In essence Kingsolver's handling of the *Bildungsroman* returns more complexity and ambiguity to the form's revisiting of a "past that must be buried, escaped, or transcended" (Stolte 63): Demon's narrative is evocative of irreconcilable tensions that suggest how life as it is lived under present conditions is untenable in essence. In a word the point is not to reintegrate into society (as David does), but to conceptualize ways of resisting the almost unassailable logic of compulsive consumption, which addiction draws its impetus from. Demon's art then becomes a powerful site of resistance against this dehumanization, for it brings a critical consciousness to bear against the desensitization and numbing that addiction perpetuates.

Neglect and Entrapment as the Ineluctable Logic of Consumption

Demon Copperhead recounts the birth of its protagonist and narrator with striking simplicity, forcing its reader to encounter the main theme of addiction from the very first page. As Demon writes, "the day [his mother] failed to show, it fell to Nance Peggot to go bang on the door, barge inside, and find her passed out on the bathroom floor with her junk all over the place and me already coming out" (*DC* 1). From the start Demon finds himself trapped within deplorable circumstances that serve to perpetuate a debilitating cycle of dependence and entrapment. Kingsolver's pessimistic evocation of a community crippled by poverty strikingly modulates her earlier, more upbeat presentation of organic belonging in novels such as *Pigs in Heaven* and *Prodigal Summer*, bringing a more concentrated focus on the social and economic factors impacting the communal ills plaguing Lee County. Indeed, Demon is himself deeply influenced by a fatalistic mindset, opining that "how would Mom know how to raise a kid? She grew up in foster care. It's inevitable she's going to raise up another total loser" (*DC* 33). Kingsolver reserves her greatest vitriol for the ways in which adults and social systems have failed to protect the vulnerable; in the words of Demon, "all the adults had gone off somewhere and left everything in our hands" (*DC* 77).

Drawing upon Dickens's ability to evoke sympathy for the children whose health and ideals have been crippled by the brutalities of economic reality, Kingsolver focuses Demon's narrative upon the fates of children—Demon, Tommy, Fast Forward, Dori, and Emmy—who have been forced to shed their innocence quickly to survive in a system engineered to exploit them. Demon's itinerant movement between foster homes adopts the structural features of Dickens's picaresque narratives only to reveal a recurring pattern of abuse and damage. This recurring motif allows Kingsolver to criticize not only the adults who have been entrusted with the duty to care for foster children, but also the functionality of the social service systems who have similarly failed to protect the vulnerable from harm. Demon, Tommy, and Fast Forward all are forced to work for a tobacco farmer, and this episode forms Demon's first encounter with addiction. Kingsolver poignantly associates addiction with consumption, emphasizing that "there lies a field that eats men and children alive" (*DC* 96), with no recourse to reimagining life outside of this dehumanizing economy. The brutality of this consumptive logic is corporeally manifested in the novel through disability, maiming, and woundedness, drawing many of the characters in Lee County together as collective victims of systemic neglect. Demon's neighbor Mr. Peg's "crushed foot" (*DC* 84) occurs as a result of him working in a coal mine before the land is used for tobacco farming, and Dori's father

Vester is ultimately killed by years of exposure to "coal dust and asbestos" (*DC* 365) in the same line of work. As Demon himself describes it, "everybody knows somebody, the near misses, the shocking falls, the guy in the wheelchair to this day" (*DC* 100) from workplace accidents involving tobacco farming. The unspoken traumas that bind together the people of Lee County manifest physically and psychologically, evincing Kingsolver's indignant outrage against economic systems that feed upon desperation and disadvantage.

That Kingsolver's critique is structural is evinced in her treatment of the opioid crisis, which damages nearly all the characters in the novel. As Kingsolver details, the rampant prescription of painkillers is legalized to the extent that they are given by "real doctors running their enterprises, the new philosophy of pain management as seen on Kent TV" (*DC* 398). The health crisis triggered by tobacco addiction, a crop that "the government used to *pay* a man to grow it, with laws about how much he could grow, and where, with price supports to make sure there was plenty and also just exactly enough" (*DC* 101), is repeated in a contemporary context, where economic logic prioritizes profit over human suffering. In this way Kingsolver demystifies addiction, exposing its horrifying economy of circulation which ultimately destroys the most marginalized and exploited. Technology aids with this exploitation, as pharmaceutical firms "looked at data and everything with their computers, and hand-picked targets like Lee County that were gold mines. They actually looked up which doctors had the most pain patients on disability, and sent out their drug reps for the full offensive," (*DC* 416) with the ease of access allowing one to "get a whole bottle of [opioids] on Medicaid, to be crushed and snorted one by one, or dissolved and injected with sheep-vax syringes from Farm Supply" (*DC* 368). Far from addiction and abuse being an unconventional topic for Kingsolver in the context of her major themes, I argue that these represent a renewed engagement with capitalistic logic and its impact on human dignity.

As Kingsolver analyzes it, addiction *is* entrapment by a dehumanizing system of production and consumption, which results in an individual being unable to break free from that which destroys and incapacitates. Indeed, the legalized system of circulation breeds other networks of exploitation and damage: Dori makes her money from filling "Vester's prescriptions at Walgreens, count out what was needed for the coming days, then come straight over here to sell the rest," making "almost two thousand bucks one time" (*DC* 398) by targeting the already addicted. The novel then presents ruthless consumption and devouring as a fact of life under political systems and institutions that have failed to protect the weak and fragile, with this vampiric urge toward destruction leaving no room for alternative conceptualizations of how social and economic justice might be possible outside of this mode of life. As Demon opines, "most families would sooner forgive you for going to prison than for moving out of Lee County" (*DC* 10), with Kingsolver's relentless presentation of this imprisonment forming the most intractable challenge to her novelistic commitment for adumbrating difference as a positive way of thinking oneself out of the status quo. We must therefore look at the novel's investments in memory, identity, and art as positive meliorative factors, folding in Demon's maturation with his ability to come to terms with not only his past, but also the collective traumas haunting Lee County.

Reclaiming Time and Identity through the Mnemonic Potentiality of Art

By choosing the quote "It's in vain to recall the past, unless it works some influence upon the present" from *David Copperfield* as the epigram to her novel, Kingsolver aptly foregrounds the transformative impact of memory upon the image of the present. As we have seen throughout her fiction, working through the traumas of the past is necessary labor, one which allows the individual to break down his or her defenses toward accepting responsibility for past decisions. In doing so we ensure that the future need not be beholden to the past as image of dead and deterministic repetition. The employment of the *Bildungsroman* signals this process of memory work, a process of uncovering the psychic sources of pain and disappointment and recognizing their impact upon identity and relationality. As Demon understands, the task of "not forgetting" is "not easy" (*DC* 7), but Kingsolver underscores how this work becomes crucial to reimagining the very bases upon which existential potentiality is negotiated.

The value of memory to social justice is highlighted by Mr. Armstrong, an unconventional teacher Demon meets during middle school. He has his class research their personal backgrounds as part of a "Backgrounds project [designed to allow students] to [find] out what type of people [they] came from" (*DC* 264). By juxtaposing this therapeutic form of retrieval and recovery against the benumbing of sensation that addiction creates, Kingsolver underscores how urgently her characters require this activation of critical consciousness, a mode that allows their own historical circumstances and dilemmas to crystallize and thereby become topics for discussion. Through reaffirming their individual histories, the students find that the present need not be enchained to the past, and the cycle of dependency can be transcended. Indeed, the critical perspective provided by historical research enables his class to understand the things "that were written about the mountaineers: shiftless, degenerate" (*DC* 265) in a new way: whereas Demon has hitherto taken these ideological concepts for the way things really are, Mr. Armstrong highlights how "they made us out to be animals so they wouldn't feel bad about taking everything we has and leaving us up the creek" (*DC* 265). Understanding the past thereby helps Demon situate his struggles within wider political forces of violence, dispossession, and systemic inequality, thereby enabling a more informed perspective about the possibilities of reconceptualizing his future as being different from the image of the past. In addition to this, learning about the past demonstrates that resistance is possible—the resources of that repressed or forgotten historical moment can be activated.

The students learn about the "Battle of Blair Mountain" (*DC* 279), a mining strike protesting deplorable working conditions. This research is significant because it allows for a dissection of the reasons why that mode of living in the past proved to be unacceptable, and the circumstances leading to the failure of that method of resistance. Through debating the topic, his students also start to learn to balance idealism with realism, thereby understanding how difficult concepts such as unemployment must be approached and tackled from multiple aspects and dimensions. Although this positive presentation of education does not dominate the novel, Kingsolver's utopian sensibility is once again reflected through her urging for awareness and critical consciousness. More important, Demon's growth in self-understanding is paralleled with his ability to use his talents to allow others to view themselves differently. As with Harrison Shepherd's talents as a novelist in *The Lacuna*, Kingsolver's artist-figures employ their media toward an aesthetic idealism that seeks to challenge intellectual complacencies.

Demon's maturation as an artist does not proceed via the conventional route of other artist-figures in literature such as Stephen Dedalus or even David Copperfield. Demon instead harnesses his "brutal talent for pictures" (*DC* 16) to become a comic strip artist. Kingsolver's depiction of Demon's comic strips emphasizes this canny attunement toward local circumstances, and how acts of superhuman heroism achieve practical benefit. In contrast to modeling his superhero persona after Batman or Superman, Demon's protagonist is surprisingly "a miner, with a pick, overalls, the hard hat with the light on the front" (*DC* 419). In this way Demon is able to fashion a local mythology and conceive of an idealism aimed at improving aspects of his community. Indeed, his hero Red Neck helps an impoverished old couple restore electrical power to their trailer home and saves children working in the tobacco fields from "the green tobacco sickness" (*DC* 429) by topping the flowers for them. Though mediated by fantasy, Demon's artistic endeavors helpfully combine the authenticity of artisanal craft (as unalienated labor) with social critique.

Kingsolver sustains an intertextual link between Demon and Holden Caulfield, the disaffected adolescent outsider of J. D. Salinger's novel *The Catcher in the Rye*, making this connection clear when Demon reflects how "that guy

Holden held my interest. Hating school, going to the city to chase whores and watch rich people's nonsense, and then you will come to find out, all he wants in his heart is to stand at the edge of a field catching little boys before they go over the cliff like I did" (*DC* 374). Despite experiencing a similar lack of connection from the people around them, Kingsolver's Demon is empathically not Holden in that he is ultimately a successful artist who forges his vision in the service of social purpose. In turn Kingsolver argues that Holden's apathy and cynicism are not attitudes her protagonist can adopt. The culmination of Demon's growth as an artist-figure is fittingly his employment of his chosen medium as a way he can abstract from the pain of the past toward objective, critical commentary about his society:

> It started with my long-ago idea of Neckbones. With Tommy's permission, I did some famous local histories through the eyes of skeletons. Knox Mine disaster, Natural Tunnel train wreck. I also messed around with the idea I'd had in my saddest days with Dori: *The Incapables*, a strip about a junkie couple trying to keep house. The guy was Crash and the girl was Bernie, two teenagers trying to raise themselves. They grilled hot dogs on their car engine while driving around to find their connect, and did household repairs with bongs and roach clips. To the best of my abilities, I made it sad and true to the laughable mess of addicted youth. Also bitter. In one of my strips, Crash is filling his pill-mill scrip and the pharmacy lady leans over to warn him, "This one's strong, hon. The Purdue rep takes it so he can sleep nights." (*DC* 520)

In its sublimation of personal trauma with addiction and sardonic commentary about society enabling this addiction, Demon has found a way his art can "push back" (*DC* 520) on life, not only by bearing witness to the authenticity of artistic inspiration, but also by providing a form of resistance against acculturated ways of living. This image of pushing back fittingly condenses an artistic impression of Kingsolver that this book has pursued: her narratives constantly challenge heteronormative modes of understanding life, human sociality, and political rhetoric, providing her reader with intimations of conceptual difference as motors of change. And yet this resistance is gentle, in that it does not seek to alienate anybody who is not amenable to readjusting their thought processes. Instead, Kingsolver solicits participation in the sharing that is fiction, crafting novels that demonstrate how participation in the perspective of the other precipitates moments of enlightenment and wonder that there *is a way out* of relentless consumption and meaningless repetition. Just as Demon ends the novel by "reclaiming [his] narrative" (*DC* 526) by standing outside of himself and his society, Kingsolver's work engages with the ethical task of defamiliarization and reclamation through testifying for silent peoples, cultures, and histories.

Possible Directions and Renewals in Reading Kingsolver Today

A fierce commitment toward social justice runs through the entire fictional output of Kingsolver; *Demon Copperhead* is her most strident denunciation of ignorance, bigotry, and the forces of inequality and discrimination that hinder people from enacting and practicing compassion and altruism. Reading Kingsolver's work is an exercise in thinking through alternatives to the loss and degradation that capitalist exploitation has accustomed us to accept as cultural rhythm: things, places, and people become objects vulnerable to commodification, use, and disposal. Her early work is as realistic about the social problems affecting disenfranchised members of the Native American community as it is idealistic about the healing benefits afforded by friendship and kinship, and the late turns toward crises in history to reveal and recover moments where change is possible, thereby implying that we do not have to accept our current way of life as the only one that can be imagined.

If it is a truism that reading literature exposes us to otherness (or othered possibilities that provide the conceptual space necessary to reconsider that which is familiar), then Kingsolver harnesses this truism to explore utopic moments of transformation, where life as it is lived can be conceived of under very different economic, political, and spiritual conditions. It has been an important argument of this book that Kingsolver maintains her commitment to reimagining difference, whether dealing with environmental issues in Appalachia or political upheaval in the twentieth century; resistance to ideological domination is both possible and necessary, in terms of a renegotiation of some of the most fundamental tenets of our collective humanity and political systems. Kingsolver's novels breathe new life into conventional philosophical questions concerning individual responsibility, existential choice, and political membership; their focuses on the interface between local and global spaces emphasize new ways that the contemporary novel can intervene in debates surrounding our place in a hypermodern, late capitalistic globalized network of signs and cultural significations.

In a political moment wherein divisions between races, classes, and cultures seem to exacerbate tensions and negate genuine communication, Kingsolver's democratizing literary imagination reaches out to embrace as many readers as possible. She is adamant that the themes in her work appeal to both the serious student and critic of ecocriticism, and the casual reader who immerses himself or herself in books as "enjoyment." In her we see an example of a contemporary novelist cannily aware not only of artistic merit and design, but also what *real* work literature can do to impact everyday attitudes. As I have argued throughout this book, Kingsolver's ideal of change functions on the level of the ordinary, and her politics is a politics of the "micro," or the quotidian. In her sympathetic understanding, science and literature do not so much stand on opposite spectrums as they complement each other—to conserve our environment and reverse degradation requires *both* empirical knowledge and the creative imagination. Indeed, if the fundamental insight of ecocriticism stresses a co-belonging that breaks down hierarchies and establishes nexuses of relationality, then these discourses are not so much competitors to truth as they are impoverished if not enriched by the framework and resources of the other.

Reading Kingsolver's work today reminds us of the existential fragility we share with other beings within the ecosphere, a fragility we have forgotten as price paid for our move into modernity. To put it simply, ecocriticism suggests that the very frames through which we understand ourselves and others in the world cannot sustain us much longer. To trouble the distinction between human and nonhuman species, and nature and culture, is to reallocate significance, integrity, and agency to objects and things around us that now cannot simply be reduced to their exchange value. In other words, ecocritical thought is a way of thinking outside of the destructive, dehumanizing impetuses of capitalist domination. To read Kingsolver is thus also to engage with a reevaluation of value, be it the significance we place in kinship ties, dietary habits, or art's political relevance. *Demon Copperhead* raises a clarion call to bring us to awareness, and to ensure that addiction to a way of life need not be binding and a pessimistic indication that we cannot resist the crushing effects of the system that suffocates and maims our better instincts and urges. Understanding Kingsolver's themes necessitates a shifting of the very foundations upon which our concepts are built—being responsible requires us to know more, feel more, and act more than what we are comfortable with. Her oft-misunderstood "didacticism" is precisely this gentle yet insistent urging, sustaining a moral vision and political impetus to her work. How we read her is relevant to the extent that ethical actions define the relevance of our beliefs and to our vision of what a "good life" is. This alone makes her fiction pressing, moving, and prescient.

WORKS CITED

Works by Barbara Kingsolver

Kingsolver, Barbara. *Animal, Vegetable, Miracle: A Year of Food Life.* New York: Harper Perennial, 2017.

———. *Animal Dreams.* New York: Harper Perennial, 2013.

———. *Demon Copperhead.* London: Faber & Faber, 2022.

———. *Flight Behavior.* London: Faber & Faber, 2012.

———. *High Tide in Tucson.* New York: Harper Perennial, 1996.

———. *Holding the Line: Women in the Great Arizona Mine Strike of 1983.* Ithaca, NY, and London: ILR Press, 1996.

———. *Pigs in Heaven.* London: Faber & Faber, 2013.

———. *Prodigal Summer.* New York: Harper Perennial, 2000.

———. *Small Wonder: Essays.* New York: HarperCollins, 2002.

———. *The Bean Trees.* New York: Harper Perennial, 2013.

———. *The Lacuna.* London: Faber & Faber, 2010.

———. *The Poisonwood Bible.* New York: Harper Perennial, 2005.

———. *Unsheltered.* New York: HarperCollins, 2018.

Secondary References

Abram, David. *Becoming Animal: An Earthly Cosmology.* New York: Pantheon, 2010.

Adorno, Theodor W., and Max Horkheimer. *Dialectic of Enlightenment: Philosophical Fragments,* translated by Edmund Jephcott. Stanford, CA: Stanford University Press, 2002.

Alaimo, Stacey. "States of Suspension: Trans-corporeality at Sea." *Interdisciplinary Studies of Literature and the Environment* 19, no. 3 (2010): 476–93.

Allen, Paula Gunn. *The Sacred Hoop.* Boston: Beacon, 1986.

Austenfeld, Anne Marie. "The Revelatory Circle in Barbara Kingsolver's 'The Poisonwood Bible'." *Journal of Narrative Theory* 36, no. 2 (2006): 293–305.

Barad, Karen. *Meeting the Universe Halfway: Quantum Physics and the Entanglement of Matter and Meaning.* Durham, NC: Duke University Press, 2007.

Barr, Alan P. "Mourning Becomes David: Loss and the Victorian Restoration of Young Copperfield." *Dickens Quarterly* 24, no. 2 (2007): 63–77.

Bate, Jonathan. *The Song of the Earth.* Basingstoke and Oxford: Picador, 2009.

Bayers, Peter. "Larry Watson's Montana 1948 and Euroamerican representations of native/Euroamerican history." *Rocky Mountain Review* 61, no. 1 (2007): 35–50.

Beattie, L. Elisabeth. "Barbara Kingsolver Interview." *Conversations with Kentucky Writers*, edited by L. Elisabeth Beattie, 150–71. Lexington: University of Kentucky Press, 1996.

Bender, Bert. "Darwin and Ecology in Novels by Jack London and Barbara Kingsolver." *Studies in American Naturalism* 6, no. 2 (2011): 107–33.

Benjamin, Jessica. *The Bonds of Love: Psychoanalysis, Feminism, and the Problem of Domination*. New York: Pantheon, 1988.

Bennett, Jane. *Vibrant Matter: A Political Ecology of Things*. Durham, NC: Duke University Press, 2010.

Boyles, Christina. "And the Gulf Did Not Devour Them: The Gulf as a Site of Transformation in Anzaldúa's *Borderlands* and Kingsolver's *The Lacuna*." *Southern Literary Journal* 46, no. 2 (2014): 193–207.

Bracke, Astrid. "'Man is the Story-Telling Animal': Graham Swift's *Waterland*, Ecocriticism and Narratology." *Interdisciplinary Studies in Literature and the Environment* 25, no. 2 (2018): 220–37.

Braidotti, Rosi. "In spite of the times: The post-secular turn in feminism." *Theory, Culture & Society* 25, no. 6 (2008): 1–24.

———. "The Critical Posthumanities; or, Is Medianatures to Naturecultures as *Zoe* Is to *Bios*?" *Cultural Politics* 12, no. 3 (2016): 380–90.

Brown, Mathieu F. "In Search of the Good Life: Portrayals of Tourism in Barbara Kingsolver's *Pigs in Heaven*." *Journal of Popular Culture* 40, no. 4 (2007): 588–600.

Browne, Victoria. "The forgetting of Mary Wollstonecraft's religiosity: teleological secularism within feminist historiography." *Journal of Gender Studies* 28, no. 7 (2019): 766–76.

Buell, Frederick. "Global Warming as Literary Narrative." *Philological Quarterly* 93, no. 3 (2014): 261–94.

Buell, Lawrence. *Writing for an Endangered World: Literature, Culture, and Environment in the U.S. and Beyond*. Cambridge, MA: Belknap Press of Harvard University Press, 2001.

Buzard, James. "*David Copperfield* and the Thresholds of Modernity." *ELH* 86, no. 1 (2019): 223–43.

Charles, Ron. "In Barbara Kingsolver's 'Unsheltered,' Trump is just the latest threat to Earth's survival," review of *Unsheltered*, by Barbara Kingsolver, *Washington Post*, October 16, 2018. https://www.washingtonpost.com/entertainment/books/.

Clark, Elizabeth A. "The Lady Vanishes: Dilemmas of a Feminist Historian after the 'Linguistic Turn'." *Church History* 67, no. 1 (1998): 1–31.

Clark, Timothy. *Ecocriticism on the Edge: The Anthropocene as a Threshold Concept*. London: Bloomsbury, 2016.

———. "Some Climate Change Ironies: Deconstruction, Environmental Politics and the Closure of Ecocriticism." *Oxford Literary Review* 32, no. 1 (2010): 131–49.

Cockrell, Amanda. "Luna Moth, Coyotes, Sugar Skulls: The Fiction of Barbara Kingsolver." In *Critical Insights: Barbara Kingsolver*, edited by Thomas Austenfeld, 173–91. Pasadena, CA: Salem, 2010.

Cohen, Robin. "Wild Indians: Kingsolver's Representation of Native America." In *Seeds of Change: Critical Essays on Barbara Kingsolver*, edited by Priscilla Leder, 145–56. Knoxville: University of Tennessee Press, 2010.

Colebrook, Claire. "Stratigraphic Time, Women's Time." *Australian Feminist Studies* 24, no. 59 (2009): 11–16.

Comer, Krista. "Sidestepping Environmental Justice: 'Natural' Landscapes and the Wilderness Plot." *Frontiers: A Journal of Women Studies* 18, no. 2 (1997): 73–101.

Coole, Diana, and Samantha Frost. *New Materialisms: Ontology, Agency, and Politics.* Durham, NC: Duke University Press, 2010.

Costello, Bonnie. *Shifting Ground: Reinventing Landscape in Modern American Poetry.* Cambridge, MA: Harvard University Press, 2003.

Croisy, Sophie. "Re-visioning Southern identity: transatlantic cultural collisions in Barbara Kingsolver's *The Poisonwood Bible.*" *Journal of Transatlantic Studies* 10, no. 3 (2012): 222–33.

Curry, Patrick. *Ecological Ethics: An Introduction.* Cambridge: Polity, 2006.

Demory, Pamela H. "Into the Heart of Light: Barbara Kingsolver Rereads *Heart of Darkness.*" *Conradiana* 34, no. 3 (2005): 181–93.

Derrida, Jacques. *Specters of Marx: The State of Debt, the Work of Mourning and the New International*, translated by Peggy Kamuf. London and New York: Routledge, 2006.

Dever, Carolyn. "Psychoanalyzing Dickens." In *Charles Dickens Studies*, edited by John Bowen and Robert L. Patten, 216–33. New York: Palgrave, 2006.

Dickens, Charles. *David Copperfield.* New York: Everyman, 1991.

Douglas, Christopher. "The Poisonwood Bible's Multicultural Graft: American Literature during the Contemporary Christian Resurgence." *American Literary History* 26, no. 1 (2014): 132–53.

Elsbree, Langdon. "Our Pursuit of Loneliness: An Alternative to the Paradigm." In *The Frontier Experience and the American Dream: Essays on American Literature*, edited by David Mogen, Mark Busby, and Paul Bryant, 31–49. College Station: Texas A&M University Press, 1989.

Evans, Rebecca. "Nomenclature, Narrative and Novum: 'The Anthropocene' and/as Science Fiction." *Science Fiction Studies* 45, no. 3 (2018): 484–99.

Fagan, Kristina. "Adoption as National Fantasy in Barbara Kingsolver's *Pigs in Heaven* and Margaret Laurence's *The Diviners.*" In *Imagining Adoption: Essays on Literature and Culture*, edited by Marianne Novy, 251–66. Ann Arbor: University of Michigan Press, 2001.

Federico, Annette. "David Copperfield and the Pursuit of Happiness." *Victorian Studies* 46, no. 1 (2003): 69–95.

Fisher, Stephen L. "Community and Hope: A Conversation." *Iron Mountain Review* 28 (2012): 26–32.

Fox, Stephen D. "Barbara Kingsolver and Keri Hulme: Disability, Family, and Culture." *Critique* 45, no. 4 (2004): 405–20.

Fraser, Alistair. "The rural geographies of Barbara Kingsolver's *Prodigal Summer.*" *Journal of Rural Studies* 35 (2014): 143–51.

Gaard, Greta, and Patrick D. Murphy. *Ecofeminist Literary Criticism: Theory, Interpretation, Pedagogy.* Urbana: University of Illinois Press, 1998.

Garrard, Greg. "Ian McEwan's Next Novel and the Future of Ecocriticism." *Contemporary Literature* 50, no. 4 (2009): 695–720.

Gersdorf, Catrin, and Sylvia Mayer. "Nature in literary and cultural studies: defining the subject of ecocriticism." In *Nature in Literary and Cultural Studies: Transatlantic*

Conversations on Ecocriticism, edited by Catrin Gersdorf and Sylvia Mayer, 9–21. Amsterdam: Rodopi, 2006.

Godfrey, Kathleen. "Barbara Kingsolver's Cherokee Nation: Problems of Representation in *Pigs in Heaven.*" *Western American Literature* 36, no. 3 (2001): 259–78.

Hanson, Susan. "Celebrating a Lively Earth: Children, Nature, and the Role of Mentors in *Prodigal Summer.*" In *Seeds of Change: Critical Essays on Barbara Kingsolver,* edited by Priscilla Leder, 251–62. Knoxville: University of Tennessee Press, 2010.

Haraway, Donna. "The Promises of Monsters: A Regenerative Politics for Inappropriate/d Others." In *Cultural Studies,* edited by Lawrence Grossberg, Cary Nelson, and Paula Treichler, 295–337. New York: Routledge, 2012.

Haynes, Roslynn D. "Bringing Science into Fiction." *ZAA* 64, no. 2 (2016): 127–48.

Hazelton, Claire Kohda. "A lesson in natural selection," review of *Unsheltered,* by Barbara Kingsolver, *The Spectator,* November 3, 2018. https://www.spectator.co.uk/article/.

Heise, Ursula K. *Sense of Place and Sense of Planet: The Environmental Imagination of the Global.* Oxford: Oxford University Press, 2008.

Himmelwright, Catherine. "Garden of Auto Parts: Kingsolver's Merger of American Western Myth and Native American Myth in 'The Bean Trees'." *Southern Literary Journal* 39, no. 2 (2007): 119–39.

Hirsch, Marianne. *The Mother/Daughter Plot: Narrative, Psychoanalysis, Feminism.* Bloomington: Indiana University Press, 1989.

Holmquist, Kate. "Emerging from a dark winter," review of *The Lacuna,* by Barbara Kingsolver, *The Irish Times,* July 23, 2010. https://www.irishtimes.com/culture/books/.

Homans, Margaret. "Adoption Narratives, Trauma, and Origins." *Narrative* 14, no. 1 (2006): 4–26.

Hornback, Bert G. *Noah's Arkitecture: A Study of Dickens's Mythology.* Athens: Ohio University Press, 1972.

Horne, Victoria. "Kate Davis: re-visioning art history after modernism and postmodernism." *Feminist Review* 110 (2015): 34–54.

Horne, Victoria, and Amy Tobin. "Open Space: An Unfinished Revolution in Art Historiography, or How to Write a Feminist Art History." *Feminist Review* 107 (2014): 75–83.

Houser, Heather. "Knowledge Work and the Commons in Barbara Kingsolver's and Ann Pancake's Appalachia." *Modern Fiction Studies* 63, no. 1 (2017): 95–115.

Hulme, Mike. *Why We Disagree About Climate Change: Understanding Controversy, Inaction and Opportunity.* Cambridge: Cambridge University Press, 2009.

Hutcheon, Linda. *The Politics of Postmodernism.* London: Routledge, 1989.

Jacobs, Naomi. "Barbara Kingsolver's Anti-Western: 'Unraveling the Myths' in *Animal Dreams.*" *Americana: The Journal of American Popular Culture* 2, no. 2 (2003): 1–13.

Jacobson, Kristin J. "Imagined Geographies." In *Seeds of Change: Critical Essays on Barbara Kingsolver,* edited by Priscilla Leder, 175–98. Knoxville: University of Tennessee Press, 2010.

———. "The Neodomestic American Novel: The Politics of Home in Barbara Kingsolver's 'The Poisonwood Bible'." *Tulsa Studies in Women's Literature* 24, no. 1 (2005): 105–27.

Jamieson, Dale. *Reason in a Dark Time: Why the Struggle to Stop Climate Change Failed —and What It Means for Our Future.* Oxford: Oxford University Press, 2014.

Jenkins, Jeffrey. "A 'deep' aesthetics of contested landscapes: Visions of land use as competing temporalities." *Geoforum* 95 (2018): 35–45.

Jones, Suzanne W. "The Southern Family Farm as Endangered Species: Possibilities for Survival in Barbara Kingsolver's *Prodigal Summer*." *Southern Literary Journal* 39, no. 1 (2006): 83–97.

Keenleyside, Heather. *Animals and Other People: Literary Forms and Living Beings in the Long Eighteenth Century*. Philadelphia: University of Pennsylvania Press, 2016.

Kerridge, Richard, and Neil Sammells. *Writing the Environment: Ecocriticism and Literature*. London: Zed Books, 1998.

Kilpatrick, Nathan. "Singing a New Song from the Conqueror's Mirror: Religious Hybridity in 'The Poisonwood Bible'." *Religion and Literature* 43, no. 3 (2011): 83–106.

Klein, Naomi. *This Changes Everything: Capitalism vs. the Climate*. New York: Simon and Schuster, 2014.

Koza, Kimberly A. "The Africa of Two Western Women Writers: Barbara Kingsolver and Margaret Laurence." *Critique* 44, no. 3 (2003): 284–94.

Kroeber, Karl. *Ecological Literary Criticism*. New York: Columbia University Press, 1994.

Kuehn, Julia. "*David Copperfield* and the Tradition of the Bildungsroman." *Dickens Quarterly* 35, no. 1 (2018): 25–46.

Leder, Priscilla. "Contingency, Cultivation, and Choice: The Garden Ethic in Barbara Kingsolver's *Prodigal Summer*." *Interdisciplinary Studies in Literature and the Environment* 16, no. 2 (2009): 228–43.

Lehtimäki, Markku. "Natural Environments in Narrative Contexts: Cross-Pollinating Ecocriticism and Narrative Theory." *Storyworlds: A Journal of Narrative Studies* 5 (2013): 119–41.

Lloyd, Christopher, and Jessica Rapson. "'Family territory' to the 'circumference of the earth': local and planetary memories of climate change in Barbara Kingsolver's *Flight Behavior*." *Textual Practice* 31, no. 5 (2017): 911–31.

Magee, Richard M. "Reintegrating Human and Nature: Modern Sentimental Ecology in Rachel Carson and Barbara Kingsolver." In *Feminist Ecocriticism: Environment, Women, and Literature*, edited by Douglas A. Vakoch, 65–76. Lanham, MD: Lexington Books, 2012.

Mayer, Svlvia. "Science in the World Risk Society: Risk, the Novel, and Global Climate Change." *ZAA* 64, no.2 (2016): 207–21.

McConnell, Anne, and Thomas Saladyga. "The Forest as Contested Landscape in Barbara Kingsolver's *Prodigal Summer*." *Geohumanities* 6, no. 1 (2020): 25–38.

McMurry, Andrew. "Ecocriticism and Discourse." In *The Routledge Handbook of Ecocriticism and Environmental Communication*, edited by Scott Slovic, Swarnalatha Rangarajan, and Vidya Sarveswaran, 15–25. London: Routledge, 2019.

Meillon, Bénédicte. "Measured Chaos: EcoPoet(h)ics of the Wild in Barbara Kingsolver's *Prodigal Summer*." *Ecozon@* 10, no. 1 (2019): 60–80.

Meire, Héloïse. "Women, a Dark Continent? *The Poisonwood Bible* as a Feminist Response to Conrad's *Heart of Darkness*." In *Seeds of Change: Critical Essays on Barbara Kingsolver*, edited by Priscilla Leder, 71–86. Knoxville: University of Tennessee Press, 2010.

Merchant, Carolyn. *Earthcare: Women and the Environment*. New York: Routledge, 1995.

Michael, Magali Cornier. *New Visions of Community in Contemporary American Fiction: Tan, Kingsolver, Castillo, Morrison.* Iowa City: University of Iowa Press, 2006.

Milne, Leah. "Choosing Africa: The Importance of Naming in 'Beloved' and 'The Poisonwood Bible'." *CLA Journal* 55, no. 4 (2012): 352–69.

Moore, Jason. *Capitalism in the Web of Life: Ecology and the Accumulation of Capital.* New York: Verso, 2015.

Moretti, Franco. *The Way of the World: The Bildungsroman in European Culture.* London: Verso, 1987.

Morton, Timothy. *Hyperobjects: Philosophy and Ecology After the End of the World.* Minneapolis: University of Minnesota Press, 2013.

Muller, Nadine. "Feminism's family drama: Female genealogies, feminist historiography, and Kate Walbert's *A Short History of Women.*" *Feminist Theory* 18, no. 1 (2017): 17–34.

Narduzzi, Dilia. "Living With Ghosts, Loving the Land: Barbara Kingsolver's *Prodigal Summer.*" *Interdisciplinary Studies in Literature and the Environment* 15, no. 2 (2008): 59–81.

Newman, Vicky. "Compelling Ties: Landscape, Community, and Sense of Place." *Peabody Journal of Education* 70, no. 4 (1995): 105–18. http://www.jstor.org/stable/1492869.

Nilanjana, Roy. "Unsheltered by Barbara Kingsolver—the certainty of home," review of *Unsheltered*, by Barbara Kingsolver. *The Financial Times*, October 19, 2018. https://www.ft.com/content/714ea070-d1f5-11e8-a9f2-7574db66bcd5.

Novy, Marianne. *Reading Adoption: Family and Difference in Fiction and Drama.* Ann Arbor: University of Michigan Press, 2005.

Ogniebene, Elaine R. "The Missionary Position: Barbara Kingsolver's 'The Poisonwood Bible'." *College Literature* 30, no. 3 (2003): 19–36.

Oppermann, Serpil. "From Ecological Postmodernism to Material Ecocriticism: Creative Materiality and Narrative Agency." In *Material Ecocriticism*, edited by Serenella Iovino and Serpil Oppermann, 21–36. Bloomington, Indiana University Press, 2014.

Park, Katherine. "Response to Brian Vickers, 'Francis Bacon, Feminist Historiography, and the Dominion of Nature'." *Journal of the History of Ideas* 69, no. 1 (2008): 143–46.

Perry, Donna. "Interview with Barbara Kingsolver." In *Backtalk: Women Writers Speak Out*, edited by Donna Perry, 143–69. New Brunswick, NJ: Rutgers University Press, 1993.

Plumwood, Val. *Feminism and the Mastery of Nature.* London: Routledge, 1993.

Rentschler, Carrie A., and Samantha C. Thrift. "Doing feminism: Event, archive, techné." *Feminist Theory* 16, no. 3 (2015): 239–49.

Riley, Jeanette E., Kathleen M. Torrens, and Susan T. Krumholz. "Contemporary Feminist Writers: Envisioning a Just World." *Contemporary Justice Review* 8, no. 1 (2005): 91–106.

Romano, Susan. "The Historical Catalina Hernández: Inhabiting the Topoi of Feminist Historiography." *Rhetoric Society Quarterly* 37, no. 4 (2007): 453–80.

Rosenthal, Debra J. "Climate-Change Fiction and Poverty Studies: Kingsolver's *Flight Behavior*, Diaz's 'Monstro,' and Bacigalupi's 'The Tamarisk Hunter'." *Interdisciplinary Studies in Literature and the Environment* 27, no. 2 (2020): 268–86.

Rubenstein, Roberta. *Home Matters: Longing and Belonging, Nostalgia and Mourning in Women's Fiction.* New York: Palgrave, 2001.

Salvatore, Anne T. "Against Platonic Authority: Collective vs. Absolute Truth in Barbara Kingsolver's 'The Poisonwood Bible'." *CLA Journal* 51, no. 2 (2007): 155–69.

Sandilands, Catriona. *The Good-Natured Feminist: Ecofeminism and The Quest for Democracy.* Minneapolis: University of Minnesota Press, 1999.

Sargent, Sarah. "Truth and Consequences: Law, Myth and Metaphor in American Indian Contested Adoption." *Liverpool Law Review* 38 (2017): 47–61.

Schillinger, Liesl. "Barbara Kingsolver's artists and idols," review of *The Lacuna*, by Barbara Kingsolver, *New York Times Book Review*, November 5, 2015. https://www.nytimes.com/2009/11/08/books/review/Schillinger-t.html.

Schultermandl, Silvia. "Motherhood and Mothering as Sites of Difference in Barbara Kingsolver's *Pigs in Heaven.*" *Journal of the Association for Research on Mothering* 8, no. 1–2 (2006): 223–32.

Scigaj, Leonard. *Sustainable Poetry: Four American Ecopoets.* Lexington: University Press of Kentucky, 1999.

Seaboyer, Judith. "Barbara Kingsolver's Singing Shepherd: *The Lacuna* as Pastoral Elegy." *Australian Literary Studies* 30, no. 2 (2015): 132–43.

Sheehan, Clair A. "Excavating *The Lacuna*: Barbara Kingsolver's allegorical understanding of America's post-9/11 world." *European Journal of American Studies* 36, no. 3 (2017): 195–208.

Simon, Irène. "David Copperfield: A Künstlerroman?" *The Review of English Studies* 43, no. 169 (1992): 40–56.

Stevens, Wallace. *Collected Poetry & Prose*, edited by Frank Kermode and Joan Richardson. New York: The Library of America, 1997.

Stevenson, Sheryl. "Trauma and Memory in *Animal Dreams.*" In *Seeds of Change: Critical Essays on Barbara Kingsolver*, edited by Priscilla Leder, 87–108. Knoxville: University of Tennessee Press, 2010.

Stolte, Tyson. "'What is Natural in Me': *David Copperfield*, Faculty Psychology, and the Association of Ideas." *Victorian Review* 36, no. 1 (2010): 55–71.

Strehle, Susan. "Chosen People: American Exceptionalism in Kingsolver's *The Poisonwood Bible.*" *Critique* 49, no. 4 (2008): 413–28.

Strickler, Breyan. "'Hemmed In': Place, Disability, and Maternity in *Animal Dreams* and *The Poisonwood Bible.*" In *Seeds of Change: Critical Essays on Barbara Kingsolver*, edited by Priscilla Leder, 110–26. Knoxville: University of Tennessee Press, 2010.

Strum, Circe. *Blood Politics: Race, Culture, and Identity in the Cherokee Nation of Oklahoma.* Berkeley and Los Angeles: University of California Press, 2002.

Sullivan, Heather I. "Dirt Theory and Material Ecocriticism." *Interdisciplinary Studies in Literature and the Environment* 19, no. 3 (2012): 515–31.

Thiele, Kathrin. "Ethos of Differentiation: New Paradigms for a (Post)humanist Ethics." *Parallax* 20 (2014): 202–16.

Tolan, Fiona. "'Everyone has left something here': The Storyteller-Historian in Kate Atkinson's *Behind the Scenes at the Museum.*" *Critique* 50, no. 3 (2009): 275–90.

Van Tassel, Kristin. "Ecofeminism and a New Agrarianism: The Female Farmer in Barbara Kingsolver's *Prodigal Summer* and Charles Frazier's *Cold Mountain.*" *Interdisciplinary Studies in Literature and the Environment* 15, no. 2 (2008): 83–102.

von Mossner, Alexa Weik. "Cli-Fi and the Feeling of Risk." *Amerikastudien* 62, no. 1 (2017): 129–38.

Wagner-Martin, Linda. *Barbara Kingsolver: Great Writers.* Philadelphia: Chelsea House, 2004.

———. *Barbara Kingsolver's World: Nature, Art and the Twenty-First Century*. New York and London: Bloomsbury, 2014.

Waldron, Karen E. "Toward a Literary Ecology through American Literary Realism and Naturalism." In *Toward a Literary Ecology: Places and Spaces in American Literature,* edited by Karen E. Waldron and Rob Friedman, 14–36. Lanham, MD: Scarecrow Press, 2013.

Weese, Kathy. "'The Eyes in the Trees': Transculturation and Magical Realism in Barbara Kingsolver's 'The Poisonwood Bible'." *Journal of the Fantastic in the Arts* 17, no. 1 (2006): 4–20.

Wenz, Peter S. "Leopold's Novel: The Land Ethic in Barbara Kingsolver's *Prodigal Summer.*" *Ethics & the Environment* 8, no. 2 (2003): 106–25.

Wetzel, Grace. "Layered Feminist Historiography: Composing Multivocal Stories Through Material Annotation Practices." *Composition Studies* 47, no. 2 (2019): 14–47.

Wheeler, Wendy. "The Lightest Burden: The Aesthetic Abductions of Biosemiotics." In *Handbook of Ecocriticism and Cultural Ecology*, edited by Hubert Zapf, 19–44. Berlin: De Gruyter, 2016.

White, Hayden. *Tropics of Discourse: Essays in Cultural Criticism*. London: Johns Hopkins University Press, 1978.

White, Jeanna Fusion. "The One-Eyed Preacher, His Crooked Daughter, and Villagers Waving Their Stumps: Barbara Kingsolver's Use of Disability in *The Poisonwood Bible.*" *South Central Review* 26, no. 3 (2009): 131–44.

Williams, Robert, Jr. *The American Indian in Western thought: The discourses of conquest*. New York: Oxford University Press, 1990.

Wrede, Theda. "Barbara Kingsolver's *Animal Dreams*: Ecofeminist Subversion of Animal Myth." In *Feminist Ecocriticism: Environment, Women, and Literature*, edited by Douglas A. Vakoch, 41–64. Lanham, MD: Lexington Books, 2012.

Yang, Karen Ya-Chu. "Female Biologists and the Practice of Dialogical Connectivity in Barbara Kingsolver's *Prodigal Summer.*" *Journal of Modern Literature* 45, no. 1 (2018): 74–86.

Zapf, Hubert. "The state of ecocriticism and the function of literature as cultural ecology." In *Nature in Literary and Cultural Studies: Transatlantic Conversations on Ecocriticism,* edited by Catrin Gersdorf and Sylvia Mayer, 49–69. Amsterdam: Rodopi, 2006.

Zapperi, Giovanni. "Women's reappearance: rethinking the archive in contemporary art—feminist perspectives." *Feminist Review* 105 (2013): 21–47.

INDEX